The Theatre of Mitchell

CW01024175

This first volume in the 4x45 series investigates the work of theatre director Katie Mitchell. Pausing to reconsider a career in progress, it engages with some of Mitchell's most recent work in the UK and Europe across theatre, opera and Live Cinema. It also takes a longer view, considering the early turns that Mitchell took at the start of her career in the late 1980s.

This volume gives full scope to the voice of the practitioner, alongside scholarly perspectives, in order to understand the work from within. Interviews with Mitchell's collaborators get inside her process – and inside the thinking of key artists who help craft the distinctive visual, aesthetic and technological forms of Mitchell's productions. Three major concerns criss-cross these contributions: the political implications of aesthetic form; the meaning of Mitchell's interest in the radical project of early Naturalism; and the influence of Europe on Mitchell's avant-garde experimentalism, which often draws on technology to open up new modes of perception and experience.

An accessible and encompassing examination of one of Europe's most celebrated theatrical talents, *4x45 | The Theatre of Katie Mitchell* is a unique resource for scholars, students and practitioners of Theatre Studies, Performance and Directing.

Benjamin Fowler is a Lecturer in Drama, Theatre and Performance at the University of Sussex who writes about directorial practice in contemporary European Theatre. Forthcoming publications include a monograph on the work of Katie Mitchell (Routledge, 2020).

4x45
Series Editor – Andy Lavender

The *4x45* project is a series of lectures, conversations and interviews in both video and print form. Each volume in the series comprises four talks from theatre and performance experts on a common theme, published in two formats:

- Four 45-minute videos available via the Digital Theatre+ platform
- A companion book collecting edited transcripts of the lectures and discussions, with an overall introduction, bibliography, and links to each video and its respective materials.

The print and video content is also supported by a blog that fosters an ongoing interactive discussion around the collection's topics and questions. The talks are given by a wide array of scholars and practitioners from across the world of theatre and performance, addressing their topics either directly to the audience or in conversation with one another.

4x45 aims to respond quickly to emerging issues and developments in all aspects of theatre, dance, and performance, reflecting and defining the important conversations across the field.

The Theatre of Katie Mitchell
Edited by Benjamin Fowler

For more information about this series, please visit: https://www.routledge.com/4x45/book-series/4X45

The Theatre of Katie Mitchell

Edited by Benjamin Fowler

Routledge
Taylor & Francis Group

LONDON AND NEW YORK

First published 2019
by Routledge
2 Park Square, Milton Park, Abingdon, Oxon OX14 4RN

and by Routledge
711 Third Avenue, New York, NY 10017

Routledge is an imprint of the Taylor & Francis Group, an informa business

© 2019 selection and editorial matter, Benjamin Fowler; individual
chapters, the contributors

British Library Cataloguing-in-Publication Data
A catalogue record for this book is available from the British Library

Library of Congress Cataloging-in-Publication Data
A catalog record for this book has been requested

ISBN: 978-1-138-60003-4 (hbk)
ISBN: 978-1-138-60005-8 (pbk)
ISBN: 978-0-429-47111-7 (ebk)

Typeset in Bembo
by Apex CoVantage, LLC

Contents

Contributors

Tom Cornford is a Lecturer in Theatre and Performance at The Royal Central School of Speech and Drama, University of London, and a director and dramaturg. Forthcoming projects include a long essay with Roberta Barker on Tyrone Guthrie for Bloomsbury's *Great European Theatre Directors* series; a special issue of *Contemporary Theatre Review*, with Caridad Svich, on Katie Mitchell, as well as a monograph: *Theatre Studios: Historicizing Ensemble Theatre-Making* (Routledge, 2018) and an edited collection: *Michael Chekhov in the Twenty-First Century: New Pathways*, with Cass Fleming (Bloomsbury, 2018). Tom was the winner, in 2017, of the David Bradby Award for Early Career Research in European Theatre.

Alex Eales is a freelance theatre designer who trained at the Wimbledon School of Art. Over the past decade he has designed extensively for Katie Mitchell, including the following operas: *The House Taken Over* (Festival d'Aix-en-Provence), *Clemency* (ROH2 and Scottish Opera), *Idomeneo* (ENO, co-designed with Vicki Mortimer) and the following theatre productions: *La Maladie de la Mort* (Théâtre des Bouffes du Nord, Paris); *Cleansed* (National Theatre, London); *Schlafende Männer, 4.48 Psychose, Reisende auf einem Bein, Glückliche Tage* and *Alles Weitere Kennen Sie aus dem Kino* (Deutsches Schauspielhaus, Hamburg); *Fräulein Julie* and *Schatten (Eurydike sagt)* (Schaubühne, Berlin); *Reise durch die Nacht* and *Wunschkonzert* (Schauspiel Köln); *The Maids* (Royal Dramatic Theatre, Stockholm); and *Say It with Flowers* and *small hours* (Hampstead Theatre Studio, London). Alex has also worked with a range of other directors at venues including the Salzburg Festival, the Danish Royal Opera and Tanztheater Pina Bausch.

Benjamin Fowler is a Lecturer in Drama, Theatre and Performance at the University of Sussex. After graduating from the MFA in Theatre Directing at Birkbeck College, University of London, he worked as an assistant director at the Manchester Royal Exchange, the RSC, the Almeida Theatre and Opera Holland Park. He now writes about theatre directing with a focus on Germany and the UK, and has published in journals including *Contemporary Theatre Review* and *Shakespeare Bulletin*. Forthcoming publications include a monograph on the work of Katie Mitchell (Routledge, 2019).

Janis Jefferies is an artist, writer and curator based at Goldsmiths, University of London. She has edited numerous books and chapter contributions on textiles, and the impact of technology on performance, literature and sound. She co-edited *The Handbook of Textile Culture* (Bloomsbury, 2015), *From Tapestry to Fiber Art: The Lausanne Biennals 1962 to 1995* (Fondation Toms Pauli Lausanne and Skira Editions Milan, 2017), and *TECHSTYLE Series 2.0: Ariadne's Thread* (Hong Kong: MILL6 Foundation, 2017). She is part of an interdisciplinary research team, based at Concordia University, Montreal, that explores *The Enchantment of Cloth* involving the dynamic of smart technology within expressive art fabrics.

Dan Rebellato is Professor of Contemporary Theatre at Royal Holloway, University of London. His research focuses on post-war British theatre, playwrighting and politics. He is the author of *1956 and All That* (Routledge, 1999) and *Theatre & Globalisation* (Palgrave Macmillan, 2009) and editor of *Contemporary European Theatre Directors* (Routledge, 2010), *The Suspect Culture Book* (Oberon, 2013), *Modern British Playwriting: The 2000s* (Bloomsbury, 2013) and the *Theatre &* series for Palgrave Macmillan. He is also a widely performed and award-winning playwright.

Kim Solga is Professor of English and Writing Studies at Western University, Canada, where she teaches theatre and performance theory and practice. Her most recent books include *Theatre & Feminism* (Palgrave Macmillan, 2015) and *A Cultural History of Theatre in the Modern Age* (Bloomsbury, 2017). With Roberta Barker, she is co-editor of the award-winning volumes *New Canadian Realisms* (Playwrights Canada Press, 2012) and with D.J. Hopkins and Shelley Orr she is co-editor of the ground-breaking *Performance and the City* (Palgrave Macmillan, 2009).

Leo Warner is the founding director of 59 Productions, a platform for developing narrative-driven projects that cross the arts-technology divide. Over the course of a decade working with director Katie Mitchell – first at the National Theatre in London and then across Europe – he pioneered methods of 'live film-making' in theatre to create a number of award-winning projects. In 2012 he led the 59 video design team on the London 2012 Olympic Opening Ceremony, directed by Danny Boyle, and in 2014 Warner led the company's first architectural projection–mapping artwork on the vast iconic 'sails' of the Sydney Opera House. In 2017 he directed Duncan Macmillan's adaptation of Paul Auster's novel, *City of Glass*, for the Lyric Theatre, Hammersmith.

Introduction

Benjamin Fowler

Rich paradoxes make Katie Mitchell's work and career a source of endless fascination. Her art is oft-labelled radical, whilst lodged in the largest and most elite mainstream institutions. It thrums with despair and anxiety, but her rehearsal room oozes with fun and delight. Frequently drawn to the high-visibility texts of the European canon, she teases out the unseen, the unsaid and the previously unthought regarding how those plays behave. She studies character (a life made linear) but shows lives lived in all their messy, complex multiplicity (only recently have plays caught up, with Alice Birch's *Anatomy of a Suicide* setting three generations across the page, realised by Mitchell in the palimpsest of a single house). Her productions unravel structures – as you'll see; *Fräulein Julie* (2010) and *Ophelias Zimmer* (2015) offer fresh slants on the source plays that expose their exclusions – only to weave new ones out of their thread. The worlds her designers build have heft, are solidly constructed, yet they summon the immaterial – a paradox at the core of Naturalism, but radically extended in Mitchell's Live Cinema work where heavy technology loads the stage, turning actors into technicians as the apparatus conjures stray, dreamlike traces of memory and desire. In these works a single consciousness takes shape through collective, collaborative labour, and recording equipment revamps *liveness*, injecting fresh doses of jeopardy and thrill. Mitchell's work holds together opposites, many of which are puzzled over in the following pages.

Another paradox: Mitchell keeps reinventing, although the work remains unmistakably Mitchell. For example, none of the productions that went into rehearsal in 2017 look anything alike: *4.48 Psychosis* was realised as a woman's walk through Hamburg (where it played), starting in her apartment at 4.48am and ending on train tracks at the city limits. To create this effect in a pitch-black proscenium, the actor Julia Wieninger walked on a treadmill that varied speed and direction as she moved through the night, her journey evoked by Jack Knowles' delicate play of light on her torso and Donato Wharton's extraordinary sound score (operators use a keyboard to 'play' her Foley-ed footsteps, taking visual cues from Wieninger's movement). *Anatomy*, mentioned earlier, was a technical rehearsal from day one in which actors practised their interlocking scenes using click-tracks composed by Paul Clark, and Pippa Meyer's stage management team routed the traffic of miraculously choreographed transitions through the Royal Court's tiny wing-space.[1] *La Maladie de la Mort*, a Live Cinema adaptation of Marguerite Duras' 1982 novel, took shape in a sweltering light-proof studio amid London's December chill – needfully so as actors in varying states of undress were working out how to film and frame carefully choreographed sex scenes for live projection on a screen above the set (a hotel room, as per the narrative). It opened in the new year in Paris.

But despite this diversity and range, everything shares the same concentration. The precision and ambition, increasingly realised as technical demand; the rigour and detail, built in intricate layers and honed by repetition, betrays a seriousness of artistic purpose that rewards close attention. Mitchell's is a very singular body of work which (that tension again) can only be communally made. It is no accident that interviews with Mitchell's collaborators bookend the volume; they get inside the process – and inside the thinking of key artists who help craft its distinctive visual and aesthetic forms – to unpack how this complex work takes place.

Its fans (of which I am one) feel so opened up by the work's intensities, its plummeting moments, its relentless insistence that we study what we might rather avoid. Mitchell's theatre, when it works well, plays with your body chemistry like music (hers is carefully scored work). It has the power to shred nerves or, as Janis Jefferies explains in Chapter 4, to make the 'hair stand on the skin'. But these same characteristics are the very things its detractors seize on as excess, as directorial 'meddling' (Kettle 2006), as distraction from the main event of well-spoken dialogue. Tom Cornford's lecture in Chapter 3 explores in depth a common case brought against Mitchell with its familiar closing argument: that her bold underlinings vandalise the text. 'I think maybe I did go awry very early on', Mitchell reflected in 2012, 'I think I tried, somehow, to do something in this culture that is like oil in water, and has been misunderstood as an aggressive, sabotaging act'. The mood has since shifted, but Mitchell spoke at a moment when her horizons in the UK were narrowing almost entirely to children's shows, as invitations from mainland Europe, along with accolades, came thick and fast. To set the scene on this conundrum, and contextualise the contributions in this volume, let's explore the turns Mitchell took 'very early on'.

The director Katie Mitchell emerged in the late 1980s, beating what remains a well-trodden path into the British theatre industry. After graduating from the English literature degree at Oxford University, where she also presided over the student drama society, Mitchell joined the Royal Shakespeare Company (RSC) as an assistant director in 1988. In 1990 she started her own company, Classics on a Shoestring, staging neglected texts at the Gate and the Old Red Lion (both fringe venues above London pubs). The RSC's artistic director, Adrian Noble, saw her *Arden of Faversham* at the Old Red Lion in 1990 which caused him to offer Mitchell her first paid work as a director: the 1991 production of Thomas Heywood's domestic tragedy, *A Woman Killed with Kindness*, at The Other Place, the RSC's experimental adjunct to the Stratford-upon-Avon mainstage.

At first glance it appears that Mitchell's background conforms with expectations as to what makes a steady pair of British directorial hands. The majority of artistic directors of the RSC and the Royal National Theatre (RNT) passed through literature degrees at Oxbridge, a pattern recently disrupted at the RNT with the appointment of Rufus Norris in 2015.[2] But Norris remains an anomaly; younger generations still have unusually high concentrations of Oxbridge graduates in their ranks (Josie Rourke, Rupert Goold, Natalie Abrahami, Robert Icke, Blanche McIntyre), and Mitchell seems to have thrived in such a milieu. At the RSC she was made an Associate Director between 1996 and 1998, responsible for programming The Other Place; under Ian Rickson she was an Associate Director at the Royal Court (2000–2004); and during Nicholas Hytner's tenure Mitchell was an RNT Associate Director for six years, beginning in 2003. Firmly embedded in these institutional structures, complete with

Royal imprimatur, Mitchell was eventually made an Officer of the Most Excellent Order of the British Empire (OBE) in the 2009 Queen's honours list for services to drama.

And yet, behind this potted biography contradictions lurk. After Oxford, something drove Mitchell to seek mentors abroad: Peter Brook, who'd fled the UK for the lung-expanding artistic freedoms of mainland Europe, agreed to meet her in Paris in 1987, and on the day of their meeting Mitchell also found Pina Bausch; that evening the 23-year-old sat, tears streaming, watching Bausch's *Nelken* (made in 1982) performed at the Théâtre du Châtelet. Unfolding on a blanket of pink carnations trampled by dancers and patrolled by attack dogs, *Nelken* opened a portal into a body of violent and poetic work, unmoored from the male gaze, that has 'haunted' Mitchell ever since. This gateway drug led to more transformative experiences in Europe in between Mitchell's RSC assisting and her directorial debut. Funded by the Winston Churchill Memorial Trust, she traversed Eastern Europe in 1989 as Socialism unspooled. Observing directors like Lev Dodin at the Maly Theatre in Russia, working in a language she accessed as privately translated whispers, Mitchell's hawk-eyed attention settled on embodied action – the extraordinary precision in physicality Dodin elicited from actors, slicing through approximations of psychological mood or cliché. The bar was set high.

From the outset, Mitchell would tangle the British text-bound tradition with something more European. Her production of *Woman Killed* (the first one, in 1991), showed clear signs with its set a square of peat (like Bausch's *Rite of Spring* [1975]) and use of candlelight and ritual song and dance lifted directly from the intense experience she shared with her movement director, Emma Rice; both had spent time immersed in the rural, almost monastic culture of the Polish theatre company Gardzienice. Such an approach would raise eyebrows in a British theatre ecology peopled by practitioners trained in literary paradigms that reinforce certain hierarchies and distributions of power, often enshrined in a male author(ity). Mitchell tackled Shakespeare only once at the RSC in 1994, and never again after the Shakespearean director and scholar John Barton informed her that 'the narrative is not clear and every single line of verse is mauled' (see Higgins 2016).

A version of the Barton note would stalk Mitchell, both in reviews and within institutions. Although Mitchell directed thirteen productions during his twelve years at the National Theatre, Nicholas Hytner (2017, 198) limits her contribution to a single page of his recent autobiography, revealing that he came to 'dread' her previews. Recognising the integrity of Mitchell's approach – but labelling hers 'a sensibility that is far outside the British mainstream' – Hytner describes how he found it increasingly hard to 'defend', apparently based on difficulties of audibility and visibility given Mitchell's 'hyperreal' (read: low) light and sound levels, her aversion to the theatrical compromise or cheat. Mitchell's major contributions to the National, under Hytner and previously, were conspicuously absent from its fiftieth birthday gala showcase broadcast in 2013. Hytner admits that he stopped employing Mitchell in his last two years, but in fact her 2011 production of *Woman Killed* (a new production of the play that was her professional debut twenty years earlier) was the final show programmed by Hytner for grown-ups. This is not to say that Mitchell's work for children (such as 2012's *Hansel & Gretel*) is second tier; she pioneered the form, part of a feminist insistence that national theatres should also cater to children and their carers.

Not enough light! It's notable that Mitchell's contemporary Emma Rice (the two share more than the experience of Gardzienice) was ousted from Shakespeare's Globe in 2017 for using too much of it – another instance of a female director transgressing the permissible, where Shakespeare's involvement caused an escalation (see Solga 2017). But accusations of misogyny are too simplistic. Some years earlier, Hytner moved to defend women who direct (including Mitchell and Rice) against negative reviews penned by – his term – 'Dead White Men' (Hoyle 2007). In calling out criticism along gendered lines, Hytner was easily rebuffed by female critics who had themselves filed negative reviews. What got occluded in the ensuing debate is the tight relationship (again) between criticism and Oxbridge; led by Billington (2007, 404–406), who often accused Mitchell of putting herself above the text, reviewers including Bassett, Coveney, Halliburton, Macaulay, Nightingale and Shuttleworth participate in a circuit of critical praxis honed at the UK's elite universities, in which the terms of reference all boil down to a literary text. In this culture, *reading* is fundamental: It is anathema not to fully see and hear a text. Tom Cornford, in Chapter 3, shows how 'operations of power within canonical texts and the perpetuation of their canonical status' interlock with 'feudal patriarchal doctrine' and other forms of structural violence. Disputes about how plays should be staged are thus never innocent; what's often at stake is the ability of hegemonic political power to flow undisturbed through our cultural circuits. It is of course typical of hegemony that its operations remain veiled, so tangible prejudice is easily disavowed in our assertions of 'taste' or a preferred way of doing things. That Hytner finally swung behind Mitchell's critics shows the tenacity of such logics. Mitchell's work – at different points for different viewers – bashes against the edges of acceptability. 'Audibility and visibility are negotiable only up to a point' (Hytner, 198) because an Oxbridge mood is the very gravity of this ecology.

This is not to say that Oxbridge determines all. Mitchell herself shows us this, widening the circle as far as Russia to let in other influences. And, indeed, what she posits as a 'wrong turn' is in fact what makes her work such a fascinating blend of lineages; to my mind, the rigour with which she *does* investigate text makes hers especially vital work, drawing on the strengths of a British tradition at the same time as testing its limits. This entire volume explores the complex artistic heritage Mitchell's work invokes. My own interview with her long-standing designer Alex Eales in Chapter 1 uncovers how even the most audacious conceptual moves remain deeply responsive to text (and deeply dependent upon collaboration). In Chapter 2, Dan Rebellato and Kim Solga debate the ways in which Mitchell's formal theatrical experiments tango with the radical project of early Naturalism, but also the later feminist critiques of the naturalist project, to launch a resuscitated and refigured Naturalism for now. Widening the frame to bring into view Mitchell's work within the highly conservative tradition of opera, Tom Cornford offers in Chapter 3 a critical reading of Mitchell that rethinks her European 'auteurism' as a highly politicised practice of aesthetic 'distraction', geared at revealing or reinterpreting aspects of the plays. Janis Jefferies' interview with Mitchell's Director of Photography, Leo Warner, rounds out the volume to reflect on the careful craft choices and processes of the Live Cinema work, the ways in which the meeting of stage and screen opens up new perceptual modes, and the inability of conventional labels to keep pace with the work and its innovative forms of collaborative labour. What makes this volume distinctive is its attempt to gather analysis that gives fuller scope to the voice of the practitioner (understanding the work from within) alongside scholarly perspectives. It also pauses to reconsider a career at what one assumes is its mid-point, featuring immediate engagement with Mitchell's most recent work at home and abroad. What criss-crosses all of these contributions is a concern with the political implications of aesthetic form, and the ways in which this develops as Mitchell herself shifts geographical position. Each contribution shows that her work renovates familiar casings from within (whether old plays, historical aesthetic styles such as Naturalism or institutions themselves), in a relentless pursuit of revelation that pushes beyond the old meanings.

There are signs that the British theatre tradition, which has shaped Mitchell's identity in so many ways, finds it easier now to evolve a place for her work. Critics with non-Oxbridge backgrounds or a training beyond literary studies, backed by a younger generation of online bloggers, show themselves readier to entertain the fluid and subtle phenomena Mitchell's work seeks to describe. In the academy, too, the topic is trending. Alongside this volume and the videos it accompanies on Digital Theatre+, a special Mitchell issue of *Contemporary Theatre Review* is in preparation, as is my own book-length study. Mitchell now teaches on an MA in Theatre Directing at Royal Holloway, and her work is on the syllabus of schools nationwide. Her increasingly vocal political and feminist agenda surely plays a part; so too may her Europeanness, which some will cherish more dearly as Brexit does its damage. But it seems that there is something in the culture now that makes us more willing to peer into dimly lit spaces, to search beyond our preconceptions for fresh illumination. You may not always hear each individual word, but – as this volume seeks in small ways to chart – Mitchell's work keeps on enlarging, adapting and extending the grammar of theatre.

March 2018

Productions

Arden of Faversham (1990), The Old Red Lion, London

A Woman Killed with Kindness (1991), Royal Shakespeare Company (The Other Place), Stratford-upon-Avon

Fräulein Julie (2010), Schaubühne am Lehniner Platz, Berlin

A Woman Killed with Kindness (2011), National Theatre (Lyttelton), London

Hansel & Gretel (2012), National Theatre (Cottesloe), London

Ophelias Zimmer (2015), Schaubühne am Lehniner Platz, Berlin

Anatomy of a Suicide (2017), Royal Court Theatre, London

4.48 Psychosis (2017), Deutsches Schauspielhaus (Malersaal), Hamburg

La Maladie de la Mort (2018), Théâtre des Bouffes du Nord, Paris

Notes

1 Pippa Meyer shared this role with Joni Carter, who managed the production once it moved into the theatre.

2 Laurence Olivier is the only other exception at the National. Although schooled in Oxford, he trained as an actor at the Central School of Speech and Drama and didn't attend university. The National Theatre became the Royal National Theatre in 1988 to mark the twenty-fifth anniversary of the company's first performance. This remains its official name, although the Royal is commonly dropped in marketing materials and on the theatre's website.

References

Billington, Michael (2007). *State of the Nation: British Theatre since 1945*. London: Faber & Faber.

Higgins, Charlotte (2016). 'Katie Mitchell, British Theatre's Queen in Exile', *The Guardian*, 14 January, www.theguardian.com/stage/2016/jan/14/british-theatre-queen-exile-katie-mitchell, accessed on 20 February 2018.

Hoyle, Ben (2007) 'Dead White Men in the Critic's Chair Scorning Work of Women Directors', *The Times*, 14 May, www.thetimes.co.uk/article/dead-white-men-in-the-critics-chair-scorning-work-of-women-directors-6jn7025295h, accessed on 20 February 2018.

Hytner, Nicholas (2017). *Balancing Acts: Behind the Scenes at London's National Theatre*. London: Jonathan Cape.

Kettle, Martin (2006). 'Hostages in the Hands of Overindulged Meddlers', *The Guardian*, 1 July, www.theguardian.com/commentisfree/2006/jul/01/arts.theatre, accessed on 20 February 2018.

Mitchell, Katie (2012). Personal interview with the author, London, 4 September.

Solga, Kim (2017). 'Shakespeare's Property Ladder: Women Directors and the Politics of "Ownership"', in *The Oxford Handbook of Shakespeare and Performance*, ed. James C. Bulman. Oxford: Oxford University Press. 104–121.

I

Immersive worlds

Designing Katie Mitchell's theatre

Alex Eales in conversation with Benjamin Fowler

Edited transcript of conversation | 27 June 2017 | Lyric Hammersmith, London

Link | digitaltheatreplus.com/4x45/katiemitchell/immersiveworlds

BENJAMIN FOWLER: Alex Eales has designed extensively for the theatre director Katie Mitchell, with 2018 marking the ten-year anniversary of their ongoing collaboration. He has, however, been part of the creative team for even longer than that – since 2003, when he was an assistant to the designer Vicki Mortimer on Mitchell's production of *Three Sisters* at the National Theatre. Working on the periphery of a number of projects at the National through the 2000s, including *Waves* (2006) and . . . *some trace of her* (2008), Alex moved to the heart of the creative team when he first designed one of Mitchell's productions in his own right: *The Maids* in Stockholm in 2008, quickly followed that same year with a production of Franz Xaver Kroetz's play *Wunschkonzert* in Cologne.

Kroetz's play doesn't feature a single line of dialogue. Instead, it consists of a series of stage directions over the course of about five pages. It depicts an evening in the life of a single, middle-aged woman, Fräulein Rasch, who returns to her apartment after a day at work. She tidies, she watches television, she prepares and eats a solitary supper, and she readies herself for bed, all the while listening to a radio show in which members of the public telephone-in suggestions for music with sentimental dedications, giving the play its English title: *Request Programme*. Finally, a few minutes into a restless sleep, Fräulein Rasch gets up and takes an overdose, and it's with this action that the play concludes.

Mitchell's production in Cologne honoured the detailed choreographic naturalism of Kroetz's dense blocks of stage directions, but it also re-envisaged the play as a technically audacious and labour-intensive spectacle that fragmented its component parts at stage level only to recombine them on a screen above the stage. Fräulein Rasch's apartment was designed as a film set, with walls that could fly in and out of position to accommodate a roving team of camera operators. There was also a string quartet in a soundproof booth on stage, which played live the classical music (in this production) that Fräulein Rasch listens to on the radio. Additional performers created all of the sound effects that accompanied the film at a downstage Foley table, and others voiced Fräulein Rasch's interior thoughts, sourced from the poetry of Anne Sexton, through a microphone. Audiences, then, were able to see these production processes at stage level alongside the film itself, which was composed and edited live, and projected onto a screen above the stage.

This production of *Wunschkonzert* was a new step in an evolving form named Live Cinema by Mitchell and her collaborators. Since *Wunschkonzert*, Alex has designed much of the Live Cinema work in Germany, including *Fräulein Julie* (2010) at Berlin's Schaubühne theatre, and *Reise durch die Nacht* (2012) in Cologne. But importantly for us today, Alex has also moved between Live Cinema and Mitchell's more naturalistic work, designing key productions including Beckett's *Glückliche Tage* [*Happy Days*] (2015) in Hamburg, Sarah Kane's plays, *Cleansed* (2016) at the National Theatre and *4.48 Psychosis* (2017) in Hamburg, and the new play by Alice Birch, *Anatomy of a Suicide* (2017), at London's Royal Court Theatre.

Alex, thank you so much for joining me today. I want to start by reflecting on the fact that for me, as someone who writes about theatre, it's really exciting to work on practitioners who are still creating and still discovering things. But I wonder what it feels like for you to momentarily step out of this collaboration with Mitchell and to reflect back on what is already an extensive body of work?

ALEX EALES: Well, it happened so gradually. I can't believe it's ten years since I did the first production with Katie, especially as, when I started working with Vicki as an assistant, I didn't really know which direction my career path was going to take. At that point, I'd made a very specific decision to do a lot of assisting, rather than trying to build up a body of smaller, touring, productions. It wasn't until I started working on Katie's productions as an assistant that I saw how I had a kind of an affinity with that work, how much I liked it, and how I could bring my own skills in a kind of detailed naturalism: that found its natural home in working with Katie. Designing my own productions alongside the work that she does with Vicki and other designers felt like a natural progression from doing the assistant work, as well as a really brilliant opportunity.

BF: I want to pick up on your description of the work's 'detailed naturalism'. I think if you're renowned for anything, it's that. . .

AE: Yes!

BF: So before we get to the Live Cinema work, let's discuss the more naturalistic proscenium shows – like *Happy Days*, like *Cleansed* – which seem to have quite a few characteristics in common. Often it appears as if we're looking through an aperture, or a frame, into a totally sealed, coherent, cohesive world on the stage. Does that reflect any rules or principles that have emerged through your collaboration with Mitchell?

AE: Yes, I think so. One of the things we're trying to create on stage is a believable environment, something that the audience can fully buy into and that they can really access in a way that takes them out of their own world, or out of the world of the theatre. We're very specifically trying to eliminate things that might remind you that you're sitting in a theatre, so we try to hide all of the theatre lights pointing down just to illuminate what's happening on stage. This might sound kind of like normal theatre practice, but I think we go an extra step. We remove as many of those markers that remind you that you're sitting in a theatre as possible. We put a ceiling on it, we try to light it with naturalistic and believable lights, either with practical lighting on stage – wall lamps, and table lamps, and pendant lighting – or with light that feels like it's natural light coming in through windows or through apertures in the rest of the set . . . even to the extent that we sometimes don't show scene changes – we'll bring a black cloth in at the front to kind of shut the audience off, so that they don't see the machinery of the theatre at work. And also, using a black cloth again, we often reveal action in motion – something that's already happening on stage – but also sometimes at the end of a production, especially with something like *Cleansed*, there's the sense that the action is continuing and we cut it off.

BF: So is the idea, then, that you're totally immersing audiences in an environment, and any kind of meta-theatrical device might risk pulling us out of it?

AE: Yes, it's an aesthetic as well as a directorial choice. That kind of immersive, completely realistic world is something that we're striving quite hard to fully recreate. We seal the world so that the audience can't leave the artifice of it.

BF: Is that always easy to do? Take a play-text like *Cleansed*, for example, which seems to be quite fragmentary in terms of its rapid progression through a series of different environments and locations.

AE: Yeah, something like *Cleansed* is actually quite difficult because, as you say, it's a number of different scenes in a number of different environments. It goes from the interior of what may or may not be a university to a patch of grass outside by a fence. At some points it's snowing, sometimes it's raining, then there's bright sunshine coming through. There's another scene where a character receives electro-convulsive therapy, so trying to package all of that into something that was believable without breaking the rhythm of the piece every fifteen minutes with a scene change was a challenge.

One of the things – and this is possibly a recurring theme – is that we try to find out where all of these things might happen. Especially with something like *Cleansed*, in which everything is so weird (e.g. people getting their hands cut off), we might ask if this happens in a believable reality, or whether it takes place in something like a dreamscape. And one of the things that we decided quite early on was that we would make *Cleansed* a dream, one that belongs to the main character, Grace, who appears on stage throughout the entire piece. We would take quite recognisable elements of dreams – for example, people have dreams where their feet are stuck to the floor and they can't move, or in which all of their teeth fall out – that we would incorporate into the piece. And therefore the nightmare (rather than the dream) of what happens during that play would all happen in one space, rather than us having to chop and do scene changes and constantly take the audience out of that world. That allowed us to coalesce all of those elements into one combined amalgam design. It might sound simplistic to put everything inside one environment or idea, but I actually feel like that clarity is about providing a structure, or a solid framework, within which to be looking at these things and not to get distracted by changing bits of scenery or this, that and the other.

BF: That's really interesting, because I think it gets to the heart of something crucial about Mitchell's work. I'm thinking now of how many reviewers have criticised her for riding roughshod over a writer's intentions, and I suppose you can see how that decision to locate all of the events in *Cleansed* inside a single environment might be seen, potentially, as something that's not following what Kane is doing in the writing. But I think it's a huge misrepresentation of Mitchell's work to suggest that it disregards the text. There's a really rigorous exploration of that text going on. I'd love to hear from you on this – what's the process when you work on a text? How do the creative decisions emerge in dialogue with some form of textual analysis, and what role do you play in that as a designer?

AE: Yes, I mean, I think it's true that we take all of our cues from the text. Even though it might seem like it, we've never really tried to shoehorn a text into an overarching high-level concept. We've only ever started with the text and built up from that. Sometimes you get to the point where there's a moment of realisation, there's a kind of epiphany, where you suddenly go, 'Oh, right, yeah, so this is the environment in which we can actually get all of these different scenes to happen. This is one composite landscape where all of these things will actually start making sense', so with something like *Cleansed*, in the stage directions, it does say that this is possibly a university environment, or there are institutional aspects to the space, and as you go through the script, you pick up on all these other little details – there are references to the university library and the university sports hall. But also, in Kane's own life, there were times when she was in institutions and in hospital, and you can see quite clearly that when she was writing the play, the troubles that she had in her own life are influencing, or they're cross-pollinating, and then you can bring all of that together and therefore put all those elements into one composite thing that seems to make it all make sense.

BF: Can we talk about another example – *Happy Days* in Hamburg – which makes some quite astonishing, quite striking departures from Beckett's directions? So, for instance, Beckett calls for Winnie to be embedded in a mound of earth; he talks about a scorched patch of grass which rises to a mound that she stands in so that it embeds her up to her waist, and then it has risen up to her neck for the second act. In your production – I mean, it's quite stunning – the material has changed to a liquid. Winnie is immersed in this dark, muddy water and you move the location so that she's trapped in a domestic interior. What was some of the thinking behind those decisions? And, again, how did they relate to the text, in that particular case?

AE: Beckett's text is very prescriptive, but we did try to hang on to as much of it as possible. There is strong sunlight referred to in the stage directions, and there are skylights above Winnie in our production so that we could get that sense of full, direct, hard light even though she's indoors. The sense that she's trapped in earth: Katie kept referring to it as 'liquid earth', and we were just looking for a reason as to why this woman is buried up to her waist – what is the situation that she's in? Katie knows Beckett's work very well, and that idea came to her because she thought there was a parallel here or something in the writing that would support it.

    I think sometimes people read that script and say, 'Oh, well it's an absurd situation. You don't need to question it, it just is. It's the way that the playwright wanted it', but I think, actually, further investigation makes you question what that situation is, and one thing that Katie has always been interested in is environmental issues – what is happening to our planet. One interpretation of this play is that it's a post-nuclear environment, or some kind of post-apocalyptic landscape. But the text is as much about imminent danger as it is about destruction that has already happened. Rather than fall into the trap of reading it as taking place *after* an event, Katie looked at it in a slightly different way, and said well, what if it is actually happening in a *changing* environment and that the situation is unstable, and therefore what are the kinds of things that are happening in our lifetime, what are the things that we relate to that could create an environment within which *Happy Days* might take place? The idea of a natural disaster, and the idea of a flooding, and the fact that Winnie is therefore trapped in what is basically water, or a mudslide, or something that has overrun her house, is just made slightly more logical. We're just being a bit clearer; we're just pushing that a little bit further in terms of our understanding of what that situation might be.

BF: And, as you're saying, not only is the thinking here responsive to Beckett's text and the progression that occurs between the acts, but it's also tying together a number of strands that have been preoccupations for you and Mitchell across different forms of work. There are Mitchell's forays into performance lectures that address environmental issues (*Ten Billion* and *2071*, for instance), but also it seems to me that *Happy Days* engages with the feminist dimensions of the practice, and an ongoing investigation of Naturalism; you know, literally bringing it inside a domestic interior. It's a really fascinating and brave choice.

AE: But it was such a strong idea, and Katie had said to me, at least eighteen months to two years before we put that show on stage, that she had had the idea of doing *Happy Days* in water. It was something that we'd been mulling over for quite some time before it actually happened. Like I said before, just seeing how this situation relates to us now rather than it being an abstract concept makes it something that people can really key into and that they really understand, and that heightens the emotional relationship between the audience and the performer, and then I think you get something much stronger from the text. Katie is always aiming for work that is clear about the relationships between people, about social history, about the way that the environment created for the characters to inhabit clarifies what is happening in the piece, and the emotional resonance that you get from that.

BF: And you mentioned then that Mitchell came to you very early on with the idea of *Happy Days* in water. Is that how it often works? Does the director offer a conceptual idea that has design implications? Or does it change project by project?

AE: Well, sometimes I come in quite early when there are no ideas about how to stage it or how to realise it, and sometimes Katie has had an idea, or she's got a thought. There are a few plays that she's worked with previously, or there are works – especially by Beckett and Chekhov – where she's got very clear ideas from her wealth of experience working on those playwrights. With *Happy Days* she was very clear about the water but that was the furthest extent of it. I did lots of sketch models of a much bleaker landscape-type version of the show, with lots of flotsam and jetsam in a post-tsunami environment. But she wanted to domesticise it and focus it right down on Winnie as a character. We kept going back to the script, looking at the details in the script. It is not full of big grand gestures or epic landscapes. When you get down into that script it's all about tiny details, it's about toothbrushes, it's about the comfort that the woman finds in the everyday. And therefore every time we had a conversation it was about getting it smaller and smaller, focusing down. So we ended up going into the domestic and reigning in the big epic conceptual sweep.

But there are some times where we literally start with an empty model box and we go, 'Oh, I don't know. How shall we do this? How shall we approach this?' With *Cleansed*, there were no ideas for it whatsoever. Katie said to me, 'It's impossible to design, good luck!'

BF: That sounds scary!

AE: Yes, but those ones are much more interesting than the ones where you have a well-trodden path of design, something where it's just going to be the same old, same old. I like working on a show where there is no tried and tested way of doing it. With *Cleansed*, other than smaller fringe or college productions, I don't think it had had a big outing since the Royal Court did it in 1998. And that was staged in a very abstract way, so our highly naturalistic, really detailed production was quite a long way from the perceived idea of what designing that show involves.

BF: Yes, you constructed an incredibly detailed, naturalistic environment. In fact, so many of these worlds that you create on stage seem to be really dense with detail and references and allusions. Sometimes it feels like they are so crammed full of things that you don't know where to look. It's almost overwhelming. We can't possibly take in or process everything inside that world. Where do you stand on that as a designer?

AE: Personally, my approach is slightly to overwhelm the audience with information. In order for it to feel naturalistic it needs overloading. As we walk around in our everyday lives, we see far too much information to process, and our brains filter out an enormous amount of information that we see as extraneous, but we recognise it as being real and believable. Therefore, when I'm designing something, in order for it to feel more real than it actually is, I put more information into it. The more detail, the more bits and pieces you include, it actually becomes more believable as a result.

The other thing – and this is kind of a personal thing – is that design can be built up by a series of unconscious or subconscious markers, and you don't quite realise that you're picking up on them when you look at a set. You don't necessarily pick it all up clearly, or recognisably, but you build up by accumulation an idea of what an environment might be. So, for example, in *Cleansed*, there are so many bits of nature in there, and the sense that nature has started to reclaim that space. There's a hole in the ceiling, and obviously water has come through, and trees have grown, and there's grass and mud. We just tried to keep adding little bits and pieces which help us understand, later in the play, why plants grow out of the floor, for example.

BF: So there's always a naturalistic causal logic at play.

AE: Yes, and the other thing is that there are an enormous amount of tiny little things, like signage, and the way that the lighting works, the light switches, sockets, the way that there is a dado-level bounce board which they have in hospital corridors to stop the gurneys from bumping into the walls, and things like that – it's about getting lots of those little bits of information, and feeding them into the design, so that people, whether they realise it or not, will recognise that space as being institutional, or more like a hospital or a school. Something they slightly recognise, but they can't quite put their finger on. There's no big sign saying 'Hospital' across the set, or something that might be more blatant. We try to build up those layers of naturalism, so that when you look at it, although you might not be able to read it all at once, you're picking it all up unconsciously. That way, you get under the audience's skin. You're passively getting them to participate, and I think that's one of the things that Katie has been looking at and developing quite specifically, although maybe not overtly. It's always about how you might get past someone's emotional barriers to what's happening on stage. Or even just the intellectual barriers that stem from sitting there and looking at something onstage and trying to distance yourself from it.

BF: It's interesting to hear how the design works through accretion in that way, and to hear you talk about how it might influence audiences subliminally, because another really dominant layer in these productions is the sound, which is doing all kinds of things both naturalistic and abstract. In coordinating the sound and the lighting and the design, how is that managed? Do all of the designers come together to conceive of this world? Or are you individual artists who are working in your own separate channels?

AE: We all come into it at slightly different stages. As the set designer, I'm always the first person, basically, to be having the conversations with Katie. That's normally to do with the schedule, and the fact that the set design needs to be handed in for construction long before anyone else's departments need to have finalised and signed off their individual parts. I'm very conscious of trying to look at a design with all of those things in mind. With sound design, for example, I've always had conversations with the sound designers [Melanie Wilson was the sound designer on *Cleansed*] about how we might get speakers into the set so that we've got sound coming from the environment, not just from speakers external to the environment. I might build ventilation grills into the set, for example, where we might hide a speaker. Or, in *Cleansed*, we actually mounted speakers onto the walls of the set that looked like they were the kind of PA system that you might have in a hospital or a psychiatric ward: high enough to be out of reach but still part of that environment. And the same with lighting. I obviously think very carefully about lighting as part of the design, because there are always going to be wall lights, or floor-standing lights, or lamps in the environment. Katie very much likes to have shows that are lit almost entirely by the practical lights themselves [rather than theatre lights], but secondary to that, I try to get in as many realistic apertures, like windows, doors, fan lights, ceiling lights, skylights – anything that we might be able to get natural-istic daylight or moonlight through, or even street-lighting. I look for some way of getting light into the space from somewhere else.

BF: Right, without revealing the theatrical source.

AE: Without revealing the source of it, yes.

BF: I'd like to move into a discussion of the Live Cinema work now. As with the work on Sarah Kane or the work on Beckett, it strikes me that we are also given access to a very sealed and cohesive naturalistic world when watching the Live Cinema work because of the screen above the stage. The screen acts like a frame, opening into a very detailed reality. But obviously in this work we also see the theatrical mechanisms – and the technological mechanisms – used to create this world laid bare at stage level. Does that pose a challenge to the notion of 'believability' that you were discussing earlier?

AE: Well, I think those projects can be viewed in a number of different ways. One way that an audience member can look at them is almost just to look at the screen, and to watch the film being delivered. I think that we layer onto that a deconstruction of that medium by laying it bare on stage. But, actually, I think sometimes it's about convincing the audience that what they're seeing is real. Sometimes the audience feels like they're being tricked, that what's happening on stage is a fake version of the creation of the film that they see on the screen above.

BF: Oh, right. Which is not the case.

AE: Which is not the case at all! It's always entirely created live on stage. In fact, we build into that system what might happen if a camera goes down. Or if a performer goes down, or if there is a cable in the way, or if for some reason we have to stop. We build into the show a way that we can stop, reset, go back to the previous setup, explain to the audience we've had a technical problem, and then we can start up again, start the machine back up.

But, actually, I feel there is . . . it's a bit difficult to explain really. There's something about seeing a live performer on stage, seeing the cameras and the artifice of that, and then seeing the performance on the screen above which is completely believable, or completely real. I think, in some way, it's the balance between those two things that helps an audience buy into that world. And I think they take the real performance from the stage and kind of overlay it onto the film above. So I think they do believe it, they do buy into it. If only, weirdly, reinforced by being able to see it in its component parts.

BF: For you, then, there's a real continuity between the more naturalistic work and the Live Cinema work? It's not a deconstruction of that way of thinking about Naturalism; it's actually enhancing it in some way, or pulling us further inside a fully realised world?

AE: Yeah, I think so. My approach has always been quite similar across these productions. The world that you see on the screen – the realistic world, the seamless, frameless world – is exactly the kind of thing that we would put on stage in a more traditional theatre piece.

BF: What do you mean by that? Because I described it in the introduction as a film set on a stage. That's not how you think about the environment that you design at stage level?

AE: Well, yes, it is a film set, but it's ostensibly the same kind of thing as it would be for a theatre set. For a theatre set, we very much talk about the fourth wall, and what you see is just the removal of that fourth wall. When we do Live Cinema, we're able to have an actual fourth wall closing off some of those film set environments so that they are completely sealed and the only way into them is with a camera. So, in that way, there is definitely a relationship between both the naturalistic theatre work and the Live Cinema work.

BF: What's the process, then, for you as a designer of a Live Cinema piece? How does that differ from a more conventional or naturalistic production?

AE: There are a lot of differences. With the Live Cinema work, just through deconstructing, just through separating those parts, you get to see how we put a film together.

It's entirely open and transparent. We have soundproof booths with either a voiceover artist or a Foley artist or a musician in them, for example. And they're in a sound-proof booth so we can control where the sound comes from, so that we can see them performing but the sound comes from the screen above.

It tends to be a black environment; we tend to put black floor down, and place the different elements in quite fixed positions on to it – we have marks all over the floor for camera positions, lighting positions, boom positions, performer positions. But actually, what we're looking at, and what Katie and I are always interested in, is what the picture is from the audience's point of view.

BF: Still within a frame, then? The whole stage?

AE: Yes, and even in the Live Cinema work we're constantly looking at what the composition is, what the stage picture is – the position of the screen, and the position of the objects on the stage, and when we reveal something on stage that the audience can see into, or a shot being set up, or when we sometimes close that down and stop the audience seeing what's being filmed on stage and divert their attention somewhere else. We're constantly looking at what the relationship is between the screen and what's happening at stage level, how the lighting makes the composition shift, and how we get things into different positions.

BF: I want to ask you about how the Live Cinema work has evolved over the years. It begins with *Waves* in 2006, which was a very fragmentary piece, but over time the environments seem to have become much more detailed and fixed and solid. And certainly in Germany these productions seem to be organised around a single protagonist, often embodied by Jule Böwe in Berlin, or Julia Wieninger in Cologne and Hamburg. I wonder what your thoughts are about how the Live Cinema form has developed, from productions like *Fräulein Julie* (2010) in Berlin to *Reise durch die Nacht* (2012) in Cologne?

AL: When it started with *Waves* at the National, the Live Cinema was very experimental in its use of the cameras. They were using things like small pieces of wallpaper attached to boards as backdrops, and they were lighting everything with angle-poised lamps. I think we've just been exploring how far we can push that materially – in terms of what we can afford to put on stage (which we've been able to do in Germany much more than we've been able to do in the UK) – but also to see what it's like to do a complete film set, rather than just filming someone with a piece of wallpaper behind them. The more we explore that, the more we find new, different, more sophisticated ways of achieving these environments.

We're always looking to do different things. With *Reise durch die Nacht*, the challenge of creating a film that looks like it's on a moving train was one of the real joys of doing that show, actually. We had moving video projection behind a train window as a backdrop, but also we created some very lo-fi bits of kit, with lights behind what really looked like spinning lampshades with slots cut into them, so that light would fall onto a performer's face and play over it as if they were going through a tunnel, or through a station. It's about finding those little bits of trickery, those little machines that we can make that help us create something, so that when you look at the screen, you go, 'Oh my God, I really believe that someone is on a train, that that train is moving, and that it's going through a station', whereas you can see on stage that, quite clearly, they are not.

BF: So you continue to develop ways of delivering the naturalistic effects of what we see in the film, but is there also something that the cameras do in terms of taking us inside a protagonist's head? They frequently seem to be showing us memory, flashback, fantasy; is the Live Cinema form allowing you to explore a single consciousness from the inside as well as from the outside?

AE: Yes, I think so. We started looking at that with *Wunschkonzert* because there's only one character in it, Fräulein Rasch, and I remember conversations with Katie and Leo [Warner, Director of Photography] in which they talked about looking at the character's world forensically, through the camera, and therefore seeing what the details were, scrutinising everything that was affecting her. There's something about that script which makes you really want to get closer, to see much more clearly what she's doing. So we spent a lot of time doing close-ups of her doing embroidery, or when she was making a cup of tea. We then discovered that this was something that was a very rich seam, and that these films can be seen as single point of view films.

We took that one step further with *Fräulein Julie*, where it was shot entirely from the perspective of Kristin the cook. In Strindberg's original play, *Miss Julie*, the focus is on Jean and Julie and their affair and Kristin is just a peripheral character, but Katie had a really brilliant idea about this peripheral character, and how she saw what was happening in the play, and what her relationship was with that. There's something really brilliant about cutting all of that – for us – extraneous text between Jean and Julie, and only looking at the bits that Kristin saw. Then, because we were so fixed on her, it gave us perfect opportunity to go inside her head for her dreams because in the play, quite famously, she falls asleep for long periods of time when other action is happening on stage. And for us those opportunities – to go inside someone's head and explore a dream landscape – are something that we're constantly looking for and referring to. So I think there has been a progression in terms of the idea of who we are looking at, why we are looking at them, and trying to make sure that we don't skip around that too much, or that we're not suddenly going somewhere else.

BF: It's really clear then that there are lots of connections between the naturalistic work and the Live Cinema productions. What I also wonder is if the Live Cinema is in turn feeding back into the more naturalistic work? I'm thinking now, based on what you've just said, about *Cleansed*, and the fact that you could read that production as showing us events entirely through Grace's eyes, because you made the decision to keep Grace on stage pretty much throughout, didn't you?

AE: Yes, that's true. Katie has a feminist perspective and she's looking very clearly through a woman's eyes at these texts in terms of thinking about how we put them on stage, and how we present them to an audience. But also – and this is possibly to do with the feminism – she's exploring these slightly lesser known or, not necessarily forgotten, but kind of ignored characters, and looking at what their perspective is. They hold just as much interest, actually, as some of the other potentially more dramatic characters. And I find it fascinating to take a classic text like *Miss Julie*, and to look at it through completely different eyes. There are plenty of people who do quite standard versions of *Miss Julie* and this was a really brilliant opportunity to look at it in a different way.

BF: Regarding the feminist aspects of the practice, many of the publicity images for these shows focus on women. I'm thinking of Francesca Woodman's photos, which have been used as posters for some of Mitchell's productions and often depict the nude female body. I wonder what your discussions are around that, especially when it comes to something like *Cleansed*, which featured quite a lot of nudity. Do you spend time discussing the representation of the female body on stage? And, if so, have there been any particularly knotty difficulties that you've had to untangle?

AE: Yes. I think Katie is very interested in the female form, from a female perspective. We're very conscious of the male gaze, and the way that women are portrayed by men, both on stage but also across media and photography and films. We try to present the body in a way that is empowering to women, but in no way trying to sugar coat things, or present the body in an overtly sexualised or pornographic way. It's been quite difficult, because we've done some shows with sex scenes in them. We've done shows where women are stripped completely bare – *Cleansed*, for example. It's a necessity of the script, and there is a gender-identity strand that runs through that narrative that has to be explored. In fact, we did both male and female nudity in *Cleansed*, if only to balance the fact that sometimes it felt like there was an emphasis on female nudity rather than male nudity. One of the things we looked at was how that might be more balanced.

BF: How did you address the woman in the box, then? Because there's a risk of paying quite voyeuristic attention to her in staging that play, isn't there?

AE: There are two different things about that. Firstly, in the text, it says that Tinker, the male character who is watching the woman, is in the box, and that he's feeding coins into a slot, and that the woman is in, potentially, a much bigger space. Actually, he's the one in a tiny booth with a small flap, able to look at this woman that he is basically putting money into a slot to watch dance. But we kind of flipped it around, so we put the woman into the box, and in a way gave her a little bit more control over the situation. When the money runs out, the box becomes opaque; it runs on a coin-operated system, when you feed money in it becomes clear, the music turns on and the woman dances, and then at a point, that token runs out and it goes opaque. We were very aware that we didn't want to expose both the performer and the character on stage more than was necessary, and that we wanted to give her a level of control over the situation as a character and, actually, put the pressure on the male character, Tinker, at that point, and his frustration, and his inadequacies, rather than make it a titillating show about a striptease.

The other thing is the fact that in our version Grace was present at those moments. Tinker has no privacy. What ended up on stage was the women's control over the situation, and Tinker's exposure and humility.

BF: You also literally show us the woman in the box side-on, don't you? We're watching Tinker looking at her, rather than just looking at her over his shoulder.

AE: Yes, absolutely. That was something that we wanted to do, just for that reason. It was about how you present that, and how we, as practitioners, might be able to manage it, and manage how the audience sees it.

BF: Before we end I want to touch on the consequences of making so much of this work in Germany. You've been engaged in lots of these Live Cinema productions, which are technically very ambitious – I described them as 'audacious' in my introduction – because they're so bold and brave in the demands that they put on performers as well as everybody else in the creative team. Over the years this work has been well supported and warmly received in Germany because of its formal experimentation. What influence, if any, has that had?

AE: The interesting thing about working in Germany is that you spend a lot of time working on set. In the UK, you get on set with three or four days of tech rehearsal and then that's it, you're done. Unless you get some previews, and then you have to take a view about how you approach previews, whether to expect to deliver a perfectly formed production in preview one or refine it in response to audience reaction. At the Schaubühne in Berlin, or the Deutsches Schauspielhaus in Hamburg, it's just taken as read that you will rehearse on set for a couple of weeks before you get anywhere close to opening a show. You gain an enormous amount. The actors get to know the environment they are inhabiting, but also we can explore how bits and pieces work specifically. You don't waste time miming that weird thing in rehearsals that you then find is two feet higher than you were expecting, or dealing with the door that doesn't stay open on its own.

With the Live Cinema work it's become more and more obvious that it's impossible to create those shows without rehearsing on the real set. You create it based on what you can see through the camera lens. And unfortunately if you're on a rehearsal set and then you end up on a real set, what you're seeing through the lens is completely different and can function aesthetically in entirely different ways. When we rehearsed *Reise durch die Nacht* we began in London, rehearsing on what was basically an MDF version of a train carriage. We came up with some really brilliant shots but basically had to re-shoot the entire show when we moved to the theatre in Cologne. In rehearsals, we couldn't tell that a door was open because everything was exactly the same colour. Whereas on the real set with the actual colours and textures you could of course see that a door was open. There was one moment where Julia [Wieninger, who played the on-screen protagonist] was listening to a Walkman as she lent up against the back wall but the reality of the train-carriage set was that the ceiling curved round at shoulder level so she couldn't sit upright. We had this beautiful shot that we couldn't replicate, so we had to change it all. So much is logistics.

BF: As a final question, then, why do you and Mitchell's other collaborators keep returning to tackle these projects given their demands and the challenges they pose? What do you get out of working with Mitchell?

AE: I enjoy both types of work, and I enjoy them balanced against each other. If I just did the Live Cinema work that might become uninteresting, but balancing it against the more conventional theatre work means that I get the best of both worlds. Katie has frequently worked with the same people. It's quite a big team now, so there are a number of set designers, sound designers and lighting designers, but we're still quite a small bunch, and I think we're all of an opinion that we want to keep striving and to come up with slightly more complicated, more interesting, or more ambitious takes on what we learnt from the last time we did it. We'll always be going, 'Oh, I remember when we did that on the last show, it would have been great if we'd had the opportunity to put that piece of scenery on a revolve', for example, which is something that turned up in *Reise durch die Nacht* from a frustration that I experienced when doing *Wunschkonzert*. I wanted to be able to rotate a piece of scenery so that the audience would get to look at it from different angles, as well as the cameras being able to get into that space. In *Reise durch die Nacht*, we were able to put the central compartment on a revolve so that we could, at times, rotate it 180 degrees, so the audience would get a different perspective on the scenery at stage level, as well as being able to see how we achieve what is produced above.

BF: You seek out challenges, then, with each new project?

AE: I think we do try to. We're our own worst enemies, always looking for more complicated and more complex solutions. There are things you learn along the way and that's one of the things I like about working with Katie on subsequent productions. For the Live Cinema work we used to roll out dance floor and mark that up with the LX tape – all the little tape marks for light and camera positions to help performers find their places on the stage. But we used to have constant awful sound issues with the cables from the cameras either making slithering noises as they were dragged across the floor at speed, or slapping when a performer would whip them to get some slack in them because they'd have to pick the camera up and run half way across the set. So on a recent production we replaced the whole thing with carpet. We were worried that the tape marks wouldn't stick, or that they would stick for a couple of days and then end up on someone's shoe, but we actually found a carpet that the longer you leave the marks on, and the more you walk on them, the more they adhere. It's a small thing, but a satisfying example for me of managing to solve a problem – a sound issue – whilst actively retaining all the properties we need logistically and practically on set for performers and technicians to do everything they need to do, whilst still having something you can roll up, put in the back of the van and take to your next venue. Or put into storage for weeks as the Schaubühne do before they bring a show back out.

Every time we do it we learn more, and I think it is an evolving form that I don't think we're anywhere near either getting bored of or testing the extremities of. I think there are more challenges ahead.

BF: Well, that's a great reminder that we're still in the middle of something. This body of work, and your collaboration with Mitchell, is very much in progress – a wonderful note to conclude on. Thank you so much, Alex, for talking with me today.

AE: Thanks very much.

Productions

Three Sisters (2003), National Theatre (Lyttelton), London
Waves (2006), National Theatre (Cottesloe), London
. . . *some trace of her* (2008), National Theatre (Cottesloe), London

The Maids (2008), Royal Dramatic Theatre, Stockholm

Wunshkonzert [*Request Programme*] (2008), Schauspiel Köln, Cologne

Fräulein Julie (2010), Schaubühne am Lehniner Platz, Berlin

Reise durch die Nacht [*Night Train*] (2012), Schauspiel Köln, Cologne

Glückliche Tage [*Happy Days*] (2015), Deutsches Schauspielhaus (Malersaal), Hamburg

Cleansed (2016), National Theatre (Dorfman), London

4.48 Psychosis (2017), Deutsches Schauspielhaus (Malersaal), Hamburg

Anatomy of a Suicide (2017), Royal Court Theatre, London

2

Katie Mitchell and the politics of naturalist theatre

Dan Rebellato and Kim Solga

Edited transcript of conversation | 22 September 2017 |
Lyric Hammersmith, London
   Link | digitaltheatreplus.com/4x45/katiemitchell/natural
isttheatre

DAN REBELLATO: Hello, I'm Dan Rebellato, Professor of
   Contemporary Theatre at Royal Holloway, University of
   London.

KIM SOLGA: And I'm Kim Solga, Professor of English and
   Writing Studies at Western University in Canada.

DR: We've both spent lots of time watching and writing
   about Katie Mitchell's work, and today we're going to be
   talking a little bit about its politics. We'll begin by each
   of us giving a short talk about one aspect of that work.
   I want to talk about Mitchell's relationship to Naturalism.

   Naturalism might seem like an odd thing to talk about
   in relation to Katie Mitchell, because people generally
   discuss her work as being radical, controversial, avant-
   garde, whereas when people think about Naturalism,
   very often what they say is that it's conservative, it's boring, it's mainstream, it's the safe option in the theatre. The

reason why I think it's important to think about Mitchell
in relation to Naturalism is that when Naturalism started,
in the last third of the nineteenth century, it was actually
all of those things that we use to describe her work: it was
absolutely experimental; it was avant-garde; it was radical,
and it was extremely shocking and controversial for its
audiences. And I think that Mitchell is trying to recover,
in a sense, some of that original radicalism of Naturalism
that has, perhaps, been lost.

I want to think about that in five different ways. There
are five different intersections between naturalist theatre
practice and what Katie Mitchell does.

The first of those I would call scenography, and I'm
thinking here about the design of Mitchell's stages and
what she makes on them. She has had, over the last
twenty-five or nearly thirty years, a series of long-term
creative partnerships with some very important designers, like Vicki Mortimer, Hildegard Bechtler and various
others, and one of the things that absolutely characterises
the kind of work that they do together is that the sets will
often look shockingly like real places you could actually
imagine going to. We are, I think, often used to going
to the theatre and expecting certain kinds of abstrac-
tions and approximations of space, but very often, when
the lights go up on a Mitchell show, you'll see a room
and you think, 'I could actually imagine somebody liv-
ing there or inhabiting that space'. Now, that's got a lot
to do with Naturalism, because one of the things that
Naturalism was famous for was a new attitude towards
scenography and, again, a kind of realism and detail in
the way that it produced the work, very often using real
material, so if you had a marble fireplace you might get a

piece of marble; if you had wooden walls you might have real wood for that, rather than a painted effect.

The reason why that's really important for Naturalism is because one of the things that naturalists wanted to do was not just *represent* the world, but they wanted to *understand* the world, and they thought that in order to understand the world and the way people behave, you have to understand the environments in which they live, because they believed our behaviour was the product of not just biological but also sociological causes. What that means is that, on stage, the set is one of the key ways in which the environment of the characters expresses itself. So, the more realistic you are about that, the more precise and accurate you can be about the effects it will have on individuals.

And we see that a lot in Mitchell's work, too, in the detail and very often – as I'll explain in a moment – in off-stage spaces. Her designers will often create spaces that the audience can't even see, but these are still part of the real world that Mitchell is trying to evoke.

The second thing I would want to talk about would be Stanislavski. Stanislavski, of course, is the great naturalist theatre director and the great champion of Chekhov, who was one of the great naturalist playwrights, but he also systematised, to some extent, his method of training his actors, in a series of books that he wrote late in his life. I'm not going to talk in any detail about exactly what that system is here, but it's probably enough to say that the aim of the Stanislavski system is to create an alignment between the actor and the character – psychologically, emotionally and physically – such that the actor can get to a point where they are using their own reactions to inhabit the character, which should create a greater sense of lived reality.

That's also very important in Mitchell's work. In the mid-1990s she was famously pulled up on the quality of her actor directing by a very skilled, Stanislavski-trained, acting teacher, and she very seriously went into thinking through the different ways in which you need to prepare actors properly under that system to create the work (see Mitchell 2009, 230). What's interesting is that you then see a whole wave of much more detailed, much more realistic acting in the work in the early 2000s, and that doesn't just affect her productions of naturalist plays, like Anton Chekhov's *Three Sisters* (2003), it also comes up when staging plays that are completely non-naturalistic, like *Attempts on Her Life* by Martin Crimp, which is a play with seventeen scenes, between which there are no obvious connections, in which the lines of dialogue are not assigned to specific speakers, where there are no indications as to space and time, and so on; it is very unlike a Chekhov play! Nonetheless, in rehearsal for her 2007 production at the National Theatre, Mitchell created an entire backstory that made sense of what the actors were doing on stage and gave them a kind of psychological reality, of a kind that Stanislavski would recognise.

The third aspect that I think is really interesting is the exclusion of the audience. Let me explain what I mean by that. In the first great naturalist theatre in the 1880s, the Théâtre Libre, the artistic director and one of its principal actors was a man called André Antoine, and he was famous for acting with his back to the audience. He did that because he thought, if you're in a room at home, you don't stand staring at the wall, you generally look towards the middle of the room, so in the theatre you should stand with your back to the fourth wall. But, of course, there's a more important aspect to that, which is that the audience is not supposed to be acknowledged. The audience is silently and invisibly observing a slice of life; and just as a scientist should not interfere with the experiments they are observing, so in the theatre the audience should not affect the performance and in that sense, they have to be ignored.

Now, actually that's something you find in a lot of Mitchell's work. Her production of *The Cherry Orchard* (2014), for example, had exactly that: people acting with their backs to the audience. Her production of *The Seagull* (2006), another naturalist play, actually got complaints because the scenes were quite dark, sometimes the actors were quite quiet, but again there was that sense that the audience has to do the work to hear this; it's not all going to be 'cheated out' for the audience. There are some productions – *The Seagull* was one of them – where the designers created off-stage rooms, unseen by the audience, where actors would go and stay in character, meaning that there are aspects of the *mise en scène* from which the audience is excluded. And in some more recent productions, like *Fräulein Julie* (2010) or *Reise durch die Nacht* [*Night Train*] (2012) – the designer created onstage rooms, in fact, where the fourth wall was complete, and the audience was therefore shut out. So, again, there's an exclusion of the audience which in Naturalism and in Mitchell's work starts as quasi-scientific objectivity (the audience/scientist as silent observer of a slice of life) but connects with and develops into an avant-garde aggression towards the audience; that we're not going to pander to you, that you are not the arbiter of artistic value.

The fourth aspect that I want to think about might seem like the opposite, which is about the primacy of the gaze. The gaze is very important for Naturalism because its practitioners held firm to the idea that we should be able to observe everything; we need to look fearlessly at everything that happens in contemporary society – no matter how shocking, no matter how revolting – and this was an iron principle of Naturalism. It was the standard answer to all the people who said that Naturalism was obsessed with filth and disease and taboo and so on; people like Émile Zola would just reply, 'We are determined to face the horrors of the world; if you don't face these horrors, how can you begin to deal with them?' And that is something else you see right across Mitchell's work.

Actually, one way you might look at it is through the use of multimedia, the Live Cinema work that has been so prominent over the last ten years. I mentioned before that in some of the recent productions there are enclosed spaces on stage, but in Live Cinema work the audience's exclusion is counteracted by their intimate access to these spaces via the roving camera and the Live Cinema screen. It actually takes us right up into the characters' faces, so we can observe the reality of human behaviour on a vastly intimate scale above the stage and we can really scrutinise the reality of people's lives and attitudes and the way that is all working out in the dramaturgy of the stage.

And the last aspect that I want to talk about is science, which I've mentioned already. I get the impression that many people assume that 'Naturalism', as a word, just means being 'natural' on stage, and actually it doesn't mean that at all, or at least it didn't originally. Naturalism was a scientific and philosophical term, which expressed the idea that human beings are wholly part of the natural world. There's nothing special about them that fundamentally distinguishes them from animals: they don't have souls; they're not blessed by God; they're not specially chosen, and so on. Even free will and human reason might be explained as the result of a biological imperative, less something causal than something caused. And that means that human behaviour can in principle be completely, scientifically understood in the same way that any other aspect of the natural world can be, and that's very important for thinking about Naturalism. It's part of the naturalist explanation for how people behave on stage.

Now, those ideas were pretty unfashionable for a lot of the twentieth century, but actually they have become, in the twenty-first century, much more fashionable again, through the rise of things like neuroscience, and neurobiology, and it's interesting to see that this is another area that Mitchell has gone into. She's shown a great interest in neuroscience, she's had conversations with scientists and writers on science like Antonio Damasio, whose ideas contributed to shows like *A Dream Play* (2005). When Mitchell adapted August Strindberg's *A Dream Play*, a play full of dream imagery, at the National Theatre, she took the idea of the play very seriously, and thought, this is a play that tries to put dreams on stage, so let's actually investigate what dreams are, and work out as objectively as possible how they should be understood and how they can be staged. I think, more generally, the

way that Mitchell talks about her work makes it often
sound quite like a scientific experiment; she's always talking about precision and clarity and lucidity; she's very
keen on observation, and you often get the sense that
she's putting together a production to set an experiment
in motion to see what then happens on the stage.

So those are five aspects that I wanted to start by talking about. Of course, what I've neglected is the aesthetics,
and of course there is an aesthetic sense that runs all the
way through Mitchell's work, right from the very beginning to the most recent, and that isn't easily brought under
the kind of scientific and realist pretentions of Naturalism.
Now, as it happens, I think that is actually also a fault line
within Naturalism, because those writers and directors
often created very beautiful plays and productions, but in
the nineteenth-century scientific view of the world, it's
not self-evident what scientific role aesthetic beauty plays.
The reason why I think it's important to think about Katie
Mitchell in terms of Naturalism is that, despite her work
clearly moving away from some of the standard tropes of
naturalist theatre, I think you could say that what she is
doing is taking the logic of Naturalist stage practice much
further, to the extent that it starts to break down some
of the conventions of theatrical Naturalism. For example,
the linearity you might expect from a naturalist play, the
visual resemblance to the world that you might be used
to, are broken down – but they are broken down because
Mitchell is radically pursuing the original naturalist theatre practices and, in the process, restoring what was radical
about Naturalism in the first place.

KS: As Dan has just indicated, Katie Mitchell's interest in Naturalism is radical; that is, it harks back to the avant-garde

movement that we call Naturalism, which, as Dan said, took shape during the nineteenth century and sought to lay bare the often very difficult conditions of social life for large swathes of the European population during a rapidly industrialising and modernising moment in history. At the same time, though, the naturalist dimensions of Mitchell's work are rooted in our moment in history, and that means that her work can often reveal paradoxes, or create contradictions as it extends, but also challenges, a traditional, historical, naturalist ethos. In the process, her work can also generate provocative questions about how theatrical form and genre can operate as political agents.

I've worked on feminist performance theory and practice for most of my career. For me, one of the most interesting ways that Katie Mitchell's naturalist practice creates paradoxes is in the way it stages women's lives and experiences. Mitchell's theatre frequently revolves around women's stories, even when the plays on which her productions are based do not. For example, in *Ophelia's Zimmer* (2015) she reframes Shakespeare's *Hamlet* through Ophelia's perspective. She spends the majority of that production following Ophelia during her off-stage moments. In *Fräulein Julie*, which Dan and I will talk about later, she retells the iconic naturalist play, *Miss Julie*, originally written by August Strindberg, through the eyes of the most neglected character in the narrative, the cook Kristin. And for *A Woman Killed with Kindness* (2011), Mitchell and her collaborator Lucy Kirkwood literally rewrote the existing text. *Woman Killed* is actually a domestic tragedy by Thomas Heywood from the early seventeenth century, but Mitchell and Kirkwood together turned it into a nineteenth-century naturalist-style narrative, placing the two female characters, Anne and Susan, centre stage – in fact, Mitchell placed them literally at the centre of the stage design, which featured interior views of two early twentieth-century houses side by side. Now, these are just three prominent examples of the woman-centred nature of Mitchell's work. In all cases, Mitchell will use her minute, detailed directorial focus on women's lives to explore the many factors – which include social, economic, historical and physiological – which impact how women are enabled or disabled by the world around them.

At this point you might be wondering about Mitchell's own politics. Around the time that she directed *A Woman Killed With Kindness*, Mitchell identified that production as explicitly feminist as she discussed it on *Woman's Hour* (2011b). Mitchell has been reticent in the past about discussing her work in feminist terms, so her willingness to own that label in relation to work like *A Woman Killed*, *Fraülein Julie* and *Ophelia's Zimmer* marks an important shift (see Higgins 2016). It's important to note here that, for a female artist, coming out as feminist can be daunting and, also, at times, quite risky. For many women in the public sphere, the term can be financially as well as professionally limiting, and potentially even dangerous. Consider, for example, how prominent feminists in the public sphere, like Mary Beard or Laura Bates, are often in the news when they are trolled online. A label like 'feminist' affects how critics read your work and how the public receives your work, and it can therefore place you, unhelpfully, in a political or aesthetic box, regardless of the work you are making or what you hope it will ultimately say. Mitchell, like many artists working on women's stories using a feminist approach, is often cautious about where and how she articulates her feminist politics. In a National Theatre platform discussion with Dan about *A Woman Killed*, for example, she was very careful about addressing the question of why she doesn't wish to direct Shakespeare again (she did so only once, in 1994, for the RSC), suggesting that perhaps Shakespeare is 'owned' by some artists more than others (by which she meant male artists, in the context of the discussion. I've recently written about this issue for a chapter in the *Oxford Handbook of Shakespeare and Performance*). At virtually the same time, however, Mitchell was happy to discuss the production's feminist sensibility in a sympathetic venue like *Woman's Hour*. This shift of tone and content from venue to venue (and audience to audience) is not indicative of 'fence-sitting' or disingenuousness on her part, note; it's an indication of how challenging it is for artists like Mitchell to balance their public profiles with their complex politics (see Mitchell 2011a; Solga 2017).

So, in her work, Katie Mitchell can be said to be both a practitioner of an avant-garde Naturalism, with its roots in the early modernist period, and a contemporary feminist artist. The collision of these two identifications is often extremely rich. It allows women's lives to be rendered in startling, precise, well-researched detail in her work and therefore to be taken seriously as substance for aesthetically rich, complex art. However, it also produces a paradox. This paradox arises because the narrative structures that govern Naturalism – that is, what we might call a naturalist *dramaturgy* – are also governed by a sense of inevitability, or social and psychological determinism.

Do you remember when Dan talked about Naturalism's roots in nineteenth-century scientific development? He was referring to the idea of humans as beings
who are part of the natural world, and thus are observable phenomena. Naturalism observes the natural world
with a careful, scientific eye, but, as a result, it also expects
the things it observes to lead to predictable outcomes –
naturalist performances are hypotheses, which come with
pre-formed expectations about results. If a woman's story
is under the microscope in a naturalist production, however sympathetic that production might be to her circumstances, her story is also likely to lead to an expected
or predictable end. Indeed, women's stories that feature
socially or psychologically predetermined endings have a
substantial place in avant-garde naturalist playwrighting.
Think, for example, of *Hedda Gabler* by Henrik Ibsen, or
Three Sisters by Anton Chekhov – though the rendering
of the female characters is complex and highly detailed,
in both cases audiences can anticipate their endings
(Hedda's unhappiness, if not death; the sisters' continued
entrapment on their rural estate) from Act One, because
this arc is built into the plays' dramaturgical structure.

For this very reason – its arc of predictability –
Naturalism has long made feminist theatre scholars uneasy.
Beginning in the 1980s these scholars began to wonder
if Naturalism inherently limited the nature of women's
stories on stage, because the genre's devotion to scientifically observable phenomena appeared to limit women's
agency, opportunity and possible outcomes. We might ask,
for example, if a story has an ending that is determined by
social circumstance, is there a place for agency, or indeed
for any kind of positive social change, within that story?

The pioneers of what we now call the feminist critique of realism and Naturalism were, among many others, Sue Ellen Case, Jill Dolan, Elin Diamond and Janelle Reinelt in the US, and Elaine Aston, Geraldine Harris and Lizbeth Goodman in the UK. Their resistance to naturalist forms had two prongs. On one hand, they critiqued the linear structure of typical naturalist dramaturgy as it drives towards that inevitable ending. On the other, they challenged the naturalist performance technique, that Stanislavskian technique Dan mentioned, that 'laminates' the body of an actor to that of her character, as Elin Diamond once famously put it, and therefore makes the differences between the body of the actor and that of the character, and between their social, cultural and embodied experiences, disappear under the rubric of a character's 'truth' (52). Unlike Bertolt Brecht's epic theatre model, in which actors step visibly in and out of character on stage in order to show audiences the different choices available to the characters within a play's reality, naturalist performance practice requires actors to become fully their characters, in order to render those characters' lives in precise detail so that they can be observed by an audience's gaze, but also so that they may make what we call a believable journey, from beginning to end of the story. Often, however, that journey's dramatic tension arises at the expense of a female character's aspirations inside the narrative. Consider Hedda committing suicide, for example, or the three sisters' failure ever to escape their humdrum lives and get to Moscow – these bad ends don't result from lack of ambition or trying, but because the naturalist, scientifically styled narrative won't achieve what it desires if they succeed in escaping the difficult social and psychological conditions the plays lift to audience view. Feminist critics analysing works of historical realism and Naturalism have noted again and again how a 'difficult' woman's story under this model is likely to end badly, or else risks being criticised as not being somehow believable.

Like the early naturalists, Katie Mitchell often focuses on the struggle of women within a harsh set of material circumstances, which means her work intersects directly with the feminist critique of realism and Naturalism. We might well ask, then: 'How do women end in the stories Mitchell tells on stage?' Well, with some frequency, they commit suicide. Now, this might seem at first a very serious problem – a return to cold 'inevitabilities' – but for a scholar like me it poses an important critical challenge. I find myself asking questions like: Does Katie Mitchell contradict her feminism when she stages a woman's self-imposed death? Should a piece of theatre that tells the story of a female character's serious struggle end with sorrow? Or is the director's, or playwright's, or actor's job to imagine a better, happier, ending for that character? On the other hand, though: If such a 'better' ending is imagined, what else gets left out of the story frame?

These questions form a bit of a catch-22. They lead us, I think, to a dead end, in which the options themselves are too limiting. There is, however, another way to unpick the problem of how a woman's story should end on stage, and that is by focusing precisely on the *how*: on the complexities of stagecraft. From *whose perspective* is a woman's story told? What *techniques* are used to reveal the contours of a female character's journey? And which aspects of that journey are included or excluded?

Is suicide framed by the production as the *only* plausible outcome for that character? Or is suicide made visible to audiences as the consequence of a series of converging material forces – forces that audiences might then debate, discuss and perhaps even change? Recent feminist readings of naturalist work by scholars like Roberta Barker (2009, 2012; see also Barker and Solga with Mazer 2013), Cary Mazer (2015), and Ben Fowler (2017) suggest that we can excavate real political potential in that work when we read more carefully the dissonance between naturalist stories and naturalist stagecraft, looking for places where the *what* and the *how* of a story's truth collide, and contradictions between them emerge.

Dan and I are now going to explore these kinds of issues, and more, in conversation. For your reference, we're going to be talking about three specific productions: *Cleansed*, by Sarah Kane, which Mitchell directed for the National Theatre in 2016; *Fräulein Julie*, by Strindberg, which was originally staged in Berlin, at the Schaubühne, in 2010; and *Anatomy of a Suicide*, by Alice Birch, which Mitchell directed at the Royal Court in London in 2017.

One last thing: while Dan and I chat, pay attention to how our conversation evolves. I'll tell you now, our conversation wasn't scripted: what you are reading is the transcript of a discussion we improvised when we recorded our video for the 4×45 series in London in September 2017. We had an outline with talking points, but that was it. What you will read below, then, is us ranging across ideas, in real time, as we collaborated together to produce new ones. This is often how academic discussion works! Scholars like Dan and I don't come up with ideas in a vacuum; we chat in the hallways at work, over email, in coffee shops or at conferences. We work consistently together to share ideas and develop new insights, to help each other to think and write better – and, of course, to help our students to learn better, as well.

***

KS: So, Dan, I wonder if we can start by chatting a little bit more about what I just called the feminist critique of realism and Naturalism in relation to Mitchell's work, specifically because both you and I were touching on the relationship between naturalist narrative and dramaturgy, and naturalist stagecraft and practice, in our opening talks. It seems to me like it would be fruitful for us to clarify a little bit the distinction between those and the way they operate in relation to the feminist critique. We might, I think, at this point, also bring in *Fräulein Julie*, which is one of the most interesting examples of naturalist dramaturgy and naturalist stage practice colliding in Mitchell's work, and is doing some of that labour of 'undoing' that you were mentioning during your talk.

DR: That's really interesting, because I was thinking, when you were talking, about this notion of inevitability that might be a rather conservative thing, that we're stuck in these patterns that we can't move out of. What's interesting though, of course, is that when these great classic naturalist plays were first produced, people didn't think they were inevitable at all, and they were outraged at the endings. Famously, when *A Doll's House* was first produced in Germany in 1880, Hedwig Niemann-Raabe, the actor playing Nora, said, 'I don't think the character would ever do that; *I* would never leave my children', and so Ibsen had to rewrite it. What's happened, of course, is that the plays have become classics, and they're now part of the European canon, and so, in a sense, they seem more inevitable, perhaps, than they actually are. So when Katie Mitchell directs *Fräulein Julie*, I think there are two things going on; one is the canonicity of the play: that it's this famous European classic that she's trying to kind of shift and get people to think about in a different way. The other thing, of course, is that August Strindberg is, famously, probably the most misogynistic playwright in history, and she's kind of wanting to challenge that as well. So she does this really interesting thing, where she takes probably the most minor character in *Miss Julie*, the maid, who kind of pops in and out of the play.

KS: And she's also the most conservative character; she's the voice of religion, which is why Strindberg dislikes her so much.

DR: That's right, absolutely, but we now see the whole thing from her point of view which, of course, means that the real drama, I suppose, or at least the central drama of Strindberg's play, is now pushed mostly off stage, and we actually watch the ordinary everyday working life of the maid. Of course, paradoxically, what's interesting is that that's a very naturalist thing to do. You take the characters that nobody really thinks about and you put them centre stage. She's kind of doing a naturalist version of a naturalist play.

KS: I was actually just thinking that, and one of the things I love about *Fräulein Julie* – and we should perhaps clarify that *Fräulein Julie* is one of the Live Cinema works that Katie Mitchell has done, so it includes a traditionally staged naturalist play in the middle of what is actually an avant-garde multimedia production, which makes it so exciting. One of the things she's doing in this piece is she's actually, I think, engaging in her own version of the feminist critique of realism and Naturalism. She's challenging Strindberg's narrative, and saying, 'I'm sorry, August Strindberg, but if you want to observe natural life, you need to look without prejudice, without ideology, at this character, Kristin, you've created: You need to observe her in her world, not simply write a series of stereotypes and call it a character', and that's one of the things that's so exciting about it. We see Kristin reciting poetry to herself; there are hints that she is struggling with an unwanted pregnancy; we see her struggling with a rivalry with Julie that she feels when she observes that Jean, her fiancé, is clearly very interested in Julie; and we see her labouring, as you said. And that's something else that Mitchell is very interested in; she's interested in the way that individual characters on stage do work. Perhaps we don't see the labour of the performer *as performer*, the way we might with Brecht, but we see the labour of servant characters, and especially female servant characters, all the time, and we're seeing those harsh social conditions that the naturalists would have been extremely interested in, but from the perspective of someone who takes women seriously as full human beings in the world.

DR: Can I pick up on something you said there? I think it might be interesting to clarify this, because if it is your argument that Strindberg is being ideological, but Katie Mitchell is being non-ideological, I'm not sure that's quite right.

KS: I think just in relation to that one character. That's a great point, though. When Strindberg talks about Kristin the cook in his preface to the play, he says some of the most abominable things imaginable about her. He says basically that she is an animal and that she is barely worthy of observation in this case. I think Mitchell takes that as a challenge and says, well, she's a human animal, and she's a human female animal; let's understand what that means in the context of the conditions you've created. There are lots of other ways that we might say Katie Mitchell wears ideological blinders, the way we all do, all the time, but that's a particular place where I think she's identified Strindberg's blind spot, and gone for it, and looked to unpick it using his own naturalist techniques.

DR: Absolutely.

KS: Is it worth talking a little bit about how the practice of Live Cinema in a show like *Fräulein Julie* collides with the naturalist acting practice that you were talking about as central to Katie's work?

DR: It's interesting. I don't know that I think it does really collide. Well, you might have some thoughts about that, but I suppose I see it more as enhancing it, in the sense that you're able to produce even more detail-rich and attentive kinds of naturalist performance, in the sense that in naturalist theatre there's always that clash between having to do life-like, detailed work, but still make yourself heard at the back of the circle, do you know what I mean?

KS: Yes.

DR: Whereas if you have a camera right up in your face, and therefore the image of your face is being projected six metres wide on a screen, you can basically do film acting; but it's live, so it's got that kind of immediate sense of experiment that theatre is probably better at doing than film, I think. But do you see a collision?

KS: I don't . . . hmmm. Maybe I don't! Maybe you've just changed my mind. I think I would identify that as a moment of paradox in Mitchell's connection to Naturalism. Having said that, I see paradox as central to naturalist practice generally, and there's actually a terrific article by the scholar Kirk Williams (2006), about this precise thing, which I always share with my students, because I think it's a brilliant reading of Naturalism's complexity. For me, one of the most exciting things about Naturalism is the fact that it pretends to be real life in order to observe real life, but it's inherently meta-theatrical, because the second you sit down in a place like the Théâtre Libre, you are fully aware of how the place has been constructed for your viewing. One of the brilliant things about Live Cinema in Katie's practice, I think, is the fact that it attunes you deliberately to that act of gazing carefully at and observing detail. It's impossible not to notice the making of the detailed cinematic object alongside your observing of it. And even though, in the moment, it's incredibly seductive, I always find myself going away and thinking about the labour of the making, the Foley table, for example, alongside the beautiful image that was created. So, as an audience member, I become politicised in my looking, simply by virtue of the fact that Mitchell is giving me both of these options: the option to look at the labour and the option to look at the product.

DR: I mentioned at the end of my opening remarks that there is this interesting fault line in Naturalism between the aesthetic and the scientific and, of course, what you get with the Live Cinema are these almost miraculously beautiful images produced on the screen. Somehow this extraordinary compositing of the image – the lighting, the angle, the sound and the set – creates these extraordinary things that you can't quite believe could be done live. And, of course, that's a meta-theatrical thought, because you're thinking all about, as you say, the labour of the people involved. And, as I say, I think that's always a productive tension in Naturalism in the first place.

KS: Yes, absolutely, and it's something Katie has used her evolving practice to really draw out. And speaking of evolving, this might be a good time for us to shift – since we've already shifted from thinking about feminism in lots of ways – to thinking about the politics of Mitchell's work more broadly. We're also slated to talk about *Cleansed* (2016), which is not a Live Cinema production – in fact it was one of the most intensively naturalistic works I've ever seen Mitchell produce. It engages with a feminist politics for me, but also queer politics, the politics of our impending ecological disaster, among many other things: torture, bad governance, a whole range of stuff. I know, Dan, that you've spent a larger amount of your career than I have thinking about Mitchell, and even working with her in different capacities. Can you talk a little bit about the evolution of her political thinking as an artist?

DR: Well, I think there are what appear to be clear phases in the work though, actually, this is going to make it sound much more like, you know, on Wednesday in this year she suddenly became, 'I'm going to be a different sort of director', and of course it isn't like that. I talk about this in more detail in an essay on Katie's work (Rebellato 2019), but broadly, I would say, she begins with what she's called a kind of anthropological phase, where she's interested in researching, very intensively, to create very detailed real worlds around the actions; she famously went to Norway to study the light, so she could get the right light for her production of Ibsen's *Ghosts* (1993), and so on. That takes you through quite a lot of the 1990s.

You then get that re-engagement with Stanislavski and a new intensity with acting. At the same time she's bringing in influences from people like Pina Bausch, the dance-theatre choreographer, and she's beginning to mix together different kinds of theatre language. So that produces a new fusion theatre, if you like, in which Stanislavski is very important, but it's also got these other kinds of high-modernist elements, I suppose you'd say. With *Waves* (2006), her adaptation of the Virginia Woolf novel, she moves into this Live Cinema period and that, I think, is where you get this real engagement with technology.

And then, more recently – although all of those previous things are still in play – you have a more explicit political engagement. In fact, I'd say you can see all of the work is driving towards this greater political engagement; there's always been a kind of feminist element in the work; there is now an increasing environmental set of concerns there too. But I think, more interestingly than just thinking about the content, there is a kind of politics of representation, which takes us back to Naturalism, a desire to get rid of the clichés of theatrical representation, to try to show people as far as possible the way they really are. And that idea runs right through the work and is expressed in lots of different ways.

KS: In *Cleansed*, that comes to a particular head because, it seems to me, the challenge of that show, for the creative team, was to create the most literal representations of torture possible, to show the audience, for example, what it would mean to cut the hands off a person in front of them. I saw *Cleansed* quite early in its run in the Dorfman Theatre, which is the small theatre at the National, and I remember a woman being taken from her seat in the stalls by members of the team after she fainted during one of the episodes, so perhaps we should talk a bit about the politics of the literal aesthetics of violence on the naturalist stage. What kind of work is that doing on an audience? And perhaps this is a minefield, but is it ethical to create imagery and sound on a stage that might generate fainting in an audience member?

DR: It's a great question, isn't it? Is it ethical to make someone faint?

KS: How close to an edge do we go in order to ask the question, 'Can we come to terms with the fact that all day, every day, in nations around the world these experiences are happening?' But we have been shielded from them by the aesthetics of representation in the media, for example, or by the way what we now call realist productions choose to present violence, which is often in a very cleansed way, ironically.

DR: Right. I mean, it's worth talking a little bit about the play, actually. Because, of course, all of those horrific events are in Sarah Kane's play.

KS: Indeed, and Sarah Kane was raked over the coals by critics for being as literal as she was in the mid-1990s – *Blasted* premiered to notoriety at the Royal Court in 1995.

DR: That's right, and also her answer to those critics was to say, 'Actually, the terrible events, I can show you the sources of them. This kind of terrible action that you think I've invented was actually a method of crucifixion in the Bosnian Civil War', for example.

KS: Yes, this is real life.

DR: The other thing that characterises *Cleansed* is several stage directions that, on one level, are impossible to do: for example, a sunflower bursting up through the floor and blossoming, a field of daffodils suddenly appearing, those sorts of things. It feels to me that what Mitchell did is decide to take these moments seriously, and figure out how they could actually happen, in a way that doesn't allow us to (a) abstract them, and just think, this is a generalised *idea* of torture, or (b) to aestheticise them and think, what a very beautiful way of representing torture. I've seen *Cleansed* a few times, and it was the first time I'd seen it and thought, 'Yes, that is probably how you would go about doing this unbelievably appalling act of torture; these are the kind of preparations you'd have to make, and this is the kind of effect it would have on the person', rather than just thinking, 'What a beautiful event or stage moment'.

KS: Absolutely. You saying that reminds me of the moment in your introductory talk when you spoke about the naturalist turn-away from the audience. We are not going to pander to you; we are not going to give you what you think you want. We are going to undertake an experiment in representation that attempts to get as close to events you normally don't gaze at as possible and see what happens. And in that sense, one might say, although even as I'm about to say this I realise the risk in saying it, that a person feeling queasy at a production of *Cleansed* in Central London in 2016, and then having to go to the lobby, sit down and drink some water is a small price to pay for a large swathe of audience members encountering something they might never have realised in their bodies and their guts before and that might, as a result, help to change their attitudes towards what we hear or see about events going on elsewhere that we tend to disregard, simply because they're not brought into close bodily proximity to us.

I have also remarked, and I know we've talked about this before, that it seemed to me, after seeing *Cleansed*, that Sarah Kane was made for Katie Mitchell, and I've long argued that Sarah Kane's roots are in realism and Naturalism, as much as they are in Beckett or the angry young men of the mid-century, precisely because she seems very interested in those aspects of the real we tend to turn away from, which is radical Naturalism in the historical sense. And Mitchell, as you just said, takes seriously the stage directions that, in the case of Kane's critics, for example, were generally dismissed as ridiculous, or the ideas about staging that seemed grotesque for the sake of being grotesque. Almost forensically, it seems, Mitchell thought to herself, or she and her team thought to themselves, 'No, let's see how we can make a sunflower burst from the ground', and, 'Let's see how we can portray the death of multiple rats on stage. Let's experiment to figure it out', and in that process she takes Kane and her labour completely seriously, in the same way that she takes Kristin the cook completely seriously, and for me that's a feminist political gesture as much as anything.

DR: I think, as well, it might be worth very briefly just talking a little bit about the difference between what we might call realism and what we might call Naturalism.

KS: Yes, absolutely.

DR: You might feel differently, but I think that Naturalism is a specific theatre movement that begins to emerge in the 1860s or 1870s and seriously flourishes in the 1880s. Realism is a kind of principle that has been around for thousands of years. You know, there are bits of Aristotle that have a realist impulse behind them, and the way I would characterise realism would just be a belief that there *is* a real world, and the theatre *can* and *should* represent it.

KS: Yes.

DR: It doesn't necessarily say anything about *how* you represent it. Naturalism is just one choice. And, of course, that's also very broad, because that means that Brecht is a realist.

KS: And Brecht identified as a realist, in fact, which a lot of people don't know.

DR: Absolutely. He's clearly not a naturalist but he is a realist, and we don't understand that if we get those things confused.

KS: No, absolutely.

DR: And even when Hamlet is talking to the actors, and he says that the purpose of acting is 'to hold as 'twere the mirror up to nature', that's a realist statement about what the theatre should be, it seems to me. In Sarah Kane's work perhaps there's a clash going on between a kind of narrow Naturalism – which is probably even clearer in her play *Blasted*, but is also there in *Cleansed* – and a broader realism that's saying the reality of the world might be in our nightmares, but we need to face that and put it on the stage. I think she took that seriously.

KS: That's a very good clarification, I think. Realism is generally connected to the idea of mimesis, which goes back to Aristotle. And, of course, there are a series of strains of practice in the history of the Western theatre that are anti-mimetic and those tend to be modernist as well. One of the very interesting things about Naturalism is that it's got a very fervent mimetic element; it's hyper-realist in some respects in that it aims for full and complete mimesis, and in that it clashed with a lot of the anti-mimetic movements, also of the modern period, but you're right that these are small strands of a larger tendency in the theatre to want to simply recreate what we understand to be our real world and, of course, the theatre invites us to debate the contents of that real world.

DR: And I think at that moment in *Cleansed*, there's a moment where one of the characters is threatened with being tortured by having a pole inserted into his rectum and pushed up through his body, and in Mitchell's production they prepared this guy in a kind of chair; there's this extraordinary detail which still haunts me, where they put this kind of cardboard bowl under him, and you realise, oh, that's to catch anything that is going to seep out of his body . . . And it was a moment of shocking realism that makes me think of things like that famous production – I'm sure you know all about this – a play by Fernand Icres called *The Butchers* that was staged at the Théâtre Libre in 1888, set in a butcher's shop, and the shocking thing they did was they hung a carcass, a side of beef, on stage. That sort of thing would never have been done before (prior to Naturalism, you'd probably just paint something, have a *trompe l'oeil* flat or backcloth or something) but now you get the shock of, presumably, the *sight* and the *smell*, and the three dimensions of it, the body of the animal on stage, that is, on one level, extraordinarily disturbing and unsettling to confront, and I think there's a real continuum between those moments.

KS: Absolutely. And I think one of the things we've been pointing to here is the way that the most intensive mimetic experiences on stage place audience members in a relationship to their bodies that they might find disquieting, that in ordinary life they might seek to repress, and that's a particularly important aspect, I think, of Mitchell's practice, of naturalist practice, insofar as it was looking to uncover the seediest elements of social life that comfortable, middle-class, late nineteenth-century men and women might not want to look at. And it also, actually, helpfully brings us back to an issue that we must revisit before we end, even though we only have a few minutes left, and that is the question of suicide in Mitchell's work.

Her latest piece, here in London at the Royal Court, was Alice Birch's brand-new play *Anatomy of a Suicide* (2017). It offered a picture of three generations of women who were haunted by a mother's suicide, and it is controversial, insofar as it staged one of the character's suicides immediately on stage. In the spirit of what I set up at the end of my introduction, I wonder if we might talk a little bit about the *how*, the staging complexities of the show. It's difficult to answer the question, 'Should a feminist show stage suicide or not?' But to ask the question, 'How is this represented and to what ends?' is a productive way into a show like *Anatomy*, I think.

DR: I think that's right, and it's interesting, because this has troubled me as well. Actually, suicides – women killing themselves – have featured in over ten of the shows that Mitchell has created in the last ten years, and you think that's a very bleak picture she's painting of the position of women.[1] I guess one response I have to that, and one of the ways I'm trying to think through what that means . . .

I'm going to mention Aristotle again, but there's that really interesting moment in Aristotle's *Poetics* (still probably the most influential thing ever written about theatre) where he says that the theatre is more philosophically valuable than history, because history just tells you what *did* happen, and the theatre tells you what *must* happen. And that, of course, is because he sees a well-written tragedy convincing you of the necessity of its actions, the inevitability of it. But it also means that the theatre contains within it a kind of generalisation, in Aristotle's model, and perhaps that thought is at work when we worry about things like these images of suicide, because we ask, 'Is that a good image of women?'

But it seems to me there's a different kind of process going on, with some of Katie Mitchell's work anyway, or at least there's certainly an impulse that's different, which is to try not to generalise at all, to be as specific as possible about particular people such that the audience shouldn't say – though it's very hard to resist this, of course – 'But this is a terrible role model for people' or 'This is a bad image of women'. You just say, 'What happened to this particular character under these particular circumstances?' Again, this is very much a naturalist way of thinking about it, and you see it in *Anatomy of a Suicide*, in that complicated textual and theatrical structure: you have three generations of women in the same family, three zones on the stage in which we see their lives and their different time periods in parallel, where we're being invited to look at the very particular effects of circumstances and history and psychology and memory (etc.) on these people, without trying to say, 'And I have therefore shown you what the female condition is now'.

KS: Yes. That's actually, I think, a really important point about this particular show. It deliberately stages, simultaneously, three different stories. They're all related, and they're all very carefully linked in the aesthetics of the show, but at the same time, they are three different stories with three different trajectories and three very different outcomes. And, as a result, we might say – and I realise that many will disagree with me here – but we might say that there's almost a Brechtian element there. We're invited to see three sets of choices, three versions of a family's reality, and to link those very precisely to social and political circumstances, as well as to choice. In the third narrative there is lots of emphasis on the character's choices, and the way she is attempting to reroute what seems like the inevitable end that her mother and her grandmother have set up for her. So there's actually something really remarkably critical about the perspective on endings in that show, even as it brings us back to what we might say is becoming a kind of Mitchell obsession with suicide as ending.

DR: I remember as well that there was another device they used in that show for the scene changes that were also costume changes, where the female protagonists in the three zones would stand on the stage and other actors (exclusively the men in some sequences) would come on with their next costume, strip them, put their new costume on, and then the show would continue. And it's a really interesting moment, because on one level, if we're generalising, it might be a way to talk about the way that men create and shape the experiences of these women, but it is also a kind of Brechtian thing that is constantly drawing attention to the choices and the labour behind the moves in the dramaturgy.

KS: Absolutely. That's probably a perfect place for us to end, actually, insofar as what you've just pointed at is the choice that we, as audience members, at Mitchell's shows but also at any show, have: we can choose to look at the stage picture through a traditional or a received mode, where we would say, 'Oh, obviously Mitchell is making a comment on gender relations in this moment', or we can take seriously the director's invitation for us to be precise in our gazes, and critical in our gazes, the way the early naturalists themselves were.

DR: Thank you.

KS: Thank you, Dan.

Productions

Ghosts (1993), Royal Shakespeare Company (The Other Place), Stratford-upon-Avon

Three Sisters (2003), National Theatre (Lyttelton), London

Iphigenia at Aulis (2004), National Theatre (Lyttelton), London

A Dream Play (2005), National Theatre (Lyttelton), London

The Seagull (2006), National Theatre (Lyttelton), London

Waves (2006), National Theatre (Cottesloe), London

Attempts on Her Life (2007), National Theatre (Lyttelton), London

Fräulein Julie (2010), Schaubühne am Lehniner Platz, Berlin

A Woman Killed with Kindness (2011), National Theatre (Lyttelton), London

The Cherry Orchard (2014), Young Vic, London

Ophelias Zimmer (2015), Schaubühne am Lehniner Platz, Berlin

Cleansed (2016), National Theatre (Dorfman), London

Anatomy of a Suicide (2017), Royal Court Theatre, London

Note

1 Since 2008 these include: *Wunschkonzert* (Schauspiel Köln, 2008); *After Dido* (Young Vic/ENO, 2009); *Fräulein Julie* (Schaubühne, 2010); *A Woman Killed with Kindness* (National Theatre, 2011); *Die Gelbe Tapete* (Schaubühne, 2013); *Wunschloses Unglück* (Burgtheater Wien, 2014); *The Forbidden Zone* (Salzburg Festival, 2014); *Ophelias Zimmer* (Schaubühne/Royal Court, 2015); *Schatten (Euridike sagt)* (Schaubühne, 2016); *Lucia Di Lammermoor* (Royal Opera House, 2016); *4.48 Psychosis* (Deutsches Schauspielhaus Hamburg, 2017); and *Anatomy of a Suicide* (Royal Court, 2017).

References

Aristotle, trans. Malcolm Heath (1996). *Poetics*. London: Penguin Classics.

Barker, Roberta (2009). 'Inner Monologues: Realist Acting and/as Shakespearean Performance Text', *Shakespeare Survey* 62: 249–260.

Barker, Roberta (2012). '"A Freshly Creepy Reality": Realist Acting and Jacobean Tragedy on the Contemporary Stage', in *Performing Early Modern Drama Today*, ed. P. Aebischer and K. Prince. Cambridge: Cambridge University Press. 121–141.

Barker, Roberta, and Kim Solga, with Cary Mazer (2013). 'Tis Pity She's a Realist: A Conversational Case Study in Realism and Early Modern Theater Today', *Shakespeare Bulletin* 31.4: 571–597.

Diamond, Elin (1997). 'Brechtian Theory/Feminist Theory: Toward a Gestic Feminist Criticism', in *Unmaking Mimesis: Essays on Feminism and Theater*. London: Routledge. 43–55.

Fowler, Benjamin (2017). '(Re)Mediating the Modernist Novel: Katie Mitchell's Live Cinema Work', in *Contemporary Approaches to Adaptation in Theatre*, ed. Kara Reilly. Basingstoke: Palgrave Macmillan. 97–119.

Higgins, Charlotte (2016). 'Katie Mitchell, British Theatre's Queen in Exile', *The Guardian*, 14 January, www.theguardian.com/stage/2016/jan/14/british-theatre-queen-exile-katie-mitchell, accessed on 8 March 2018.

Mazer, Cary (2015). *Double Shakespeares: Emotional-Realist Acting and Contemporary Performance*. Madison, NJ: Fairleigh Dickinson University Press.

Mitchell, Katie (2009). *The Director's Craft: A Handbook for the Theatre*. Abingdon: Routledge.

Mitchell, Katie (2011a). 'Platform Talk: A Woman Killed with Kindness', National Theatre, London, 22 August, Audio recording, RNT digital archive, accessed on 5 December 2011.

Mitchell, Katie, and Hannah Crawford (2011b). 'Interview', *Woman's Hour*, BBC Radio 4, 19 July, www.bbc.co.uk/programmes/b012l1y8, accessed on 8 March 2018.

Rebellato, Dan (2019). 'Katie Mitchell: Learning from Europe', in *Contemporary European Theatre Directors*, ed. Maria M. Delgado and Dan Rebellato. 2nd ed. Abingdon: Routledge.

Solga, Kim (2017). 'Shakespeare's Property Ladder: Women Directors and the Politics of "Ownership"', in *The Oxford Handbook of Shakespeare and Performance*, ed. James C. Bulman. Oxford: Oxford University Press. 104–121.

Williams, Kirk (2006). 'Anti-Theatricality and the Limits of Naturalism', in *Against Theatre: Creative Destructions on the Modernist Stage*, ed. Alan Ackerman and Martin Puchner. Basingstoke: Palgrave MacMillan. 95–111.

3

Willful distraction

Katie Mitchell, auteurism and the canon

Tom Cornford

Edited transcript of a lecture | 6th July 2017 | Lyric Hammersmith, London

Link | digitaltheatreplus.com/4x45/katiemitchell/wilfuldistraction

Willfulness

The opening of Katie Mitchell's Royal Opera House production of *Lucia di Lammermoor* in April 2016 was, unusually, considered worthy of mention on the following morning's *Today* programme. Widespread booing was reported, and *The Guardian* critic Charlotte Higgins described 'a real feeling of division in the audience' over Mitchell and her designer Vicki Mortimer's decision to use a form of split-screen staging to expose the operations and consequences of patriarchal abuse in the narrative that are otherwise excluded from the audience's direct awareness by being conducted off-stage (BBC News 2016). These interpolated scenes, which included the staging of Lucia's murder of her husband, had been considered by the Royal Opera House's management to be sufficiently concerning to warrant the sending of an email to those who had booked for the production, warning of 'scenes that feature sexual acts portrayed on stage, and other scenes that – as you might expect from the story of Lucia – feature violence'. The Opera House sought to reassure its customers that 'If there are any members of your party who you feel may be upset by such scenes then please email us [...] and we will, of course, discuss suitable arrangements' (Royal Opera House 2016). Mitchell's interpolations were widely criticised in reviews of the opera. 'A lot of thought has gone into Katie Mitchell's staging', wrote Rupert Christiansen (2016), 'most of it misguided'.

Mitchell has long had a reputation with British theatre critics for willfulness. In 2007, reviews of her production of Euripides' *Women of Troy* at the National Theatre united voices from opposite sides of the political spectrum in approbation. In *The Guardian*, Michael Billington (2007) expressed his regret that whereas 'Once [Mitchell] was content to realise an author's text, now she has become an auteur whose signature is on every moment of a production'. The 'lament against auteurism' has figured prominently in Billington's writing, as Dan Rebellato (2010, 317) has observed, and has been directed particularly at Mitchell whom he described, also in 2007, as 'the controlling figure and ultimate auteur in a continental European tradition'. Billington's argument was echoed in more vociferous terms in Charles Spencer's (2007) *Daily Telegraph* review of *Women of Troy*. He argued that Mitchell's 'primary aim isn't to serve the dead author', her 'particular specialty [...] is smashing up the classics [...] using what she needs, discarding what doesn't suit her, and leaving her grubby fingerprints all over whatever survives of the original masterpiece'. Spencer suggested that this is 'common practice among the directorial auteurs of Europe' but pronounced himself relieved that 'this overweening arrogance is mercifully less often seen in Britain'. Rebellato argues, on the basis of this evidence, that 'Mitchell's work has a sensibility and a set of priorities that fit awkwardly into the institutional structures or critical consensus that surround British theatrical practice. Put simply', he writes, 'Katie Mitchell is too European for some British tastes' (319).

No doubt this argument is correct, but I think it is not merely a matter of taste. Or, more precisely, there is more at stake in 'British tastes' than merely what people happen to like. I argue here that Sara Ahmed's idea of the 'willful subject' can help us to probe beneath the bluff, dismissive xenophobia and misogyny we find in Billington and Spencer's accounts of Mitchell's work. Ahmed's concept of willfulness, I argue, brings into focus what is at stake politically in the 'institutional structures' and 'critical consensus' that have shaped the presumed 'British tastes' by whose standards Mitchell is deemed a joyless, overweening, cultural vandal. Ahmed's idea of 'willfulness' also enables us to see distraction as a political strategy that exposes the operations of power within canonical texts and the perpetuation of their canonical status. I begin by tracing the history of the term 'auteur', which is the principal accusation of Mitchell's opponents, and go on to read Mitchell's interventions into the dramatic canon not as vandalism, but as willful distractions from the conservative agenda it commonly represents. As the idea of a 'canon' was consolidated in the nineteenth century, I offer, as examples, three texts that emerged from that time, and are now considered canonical: Donizetti's *Lucia di Lammermoor*, Strindberg's *Miss Julie* and Chekhov's *The Cherry Orchard*. I conclude with a cautionary note about the dangerous security of willfulness, and its capacity to distract those, such as Mitchell, who choose to adopt its position.

Auteurism

What does it mean to label Katie Mitchell an auteur? The term 'auteur' began in the cinema, where it was first espoused by French director Francois Truffaut in the 1950s. It refers to the idea that the director should be considered the primary author of the film and it continues, for example, in the convention of assigning films in their credits to directors (rather than producers, authors, cinematographers, editors, or to collective authorship). At this point, I'd like to draw your attention to the fact that this section of my talk is unusual in its dependence upon the work of male theorists. The reason for that is simple: Auteurism is, and has always been, a male theory. Just as marriage traditionally collapsed a wife's identify into that of her husband, auterism requires that the creative process is absorbed into the figure of the auteur. And just as the medieval principle of primogeniture asserts the right of the first male child to inherit titles and property, the auteur, as primary author, is placed so as to receive by far the greatest credit for a creative work. Auteurism is thus problematically aligned with feudal patriarchal doctrine. This is ironically revealing in relation to Billington and Spencer's accusation, because they have levelled it principally at women. Alongside Mitchell, Spencer's review indicts Deborah Warner and Emma Rice, and Billington (2009) has likewise accused Rice of auteurism. To unpick the power relations at work in this process in which (male) critics are accusing (mainly female) artists of auteurism for reimagining the works of (male) authors, we may turn to the work of feminist scholar Sara Ahmed.

Ahmed writes in her book *Willful Subjects* that 'willfulness is used to explain errors of will – unreasonable or perverted wills – as faults of character' (Spencer diagnoses Mitchell's will to reimagine *Women of Troy* as 'overweening arrogance', for instance). Ahmed argues that 'willfulness can thus be understood, in the first instance, as an attribution to a subject of will's error' (2014, 4). Willfulness, as the plural of Ahmed's title proposes – can also be many other things, but they tend to exist at odds with the will of power. 'One way of thinking of the sovereign will', Ahmed writes, 'is the right to determine whose wills are willful wills'. She goes on to observe, however, that 'a rebellion against tyranny might involve those named as willful renaming the sovereign will as willful will, the sovereign as tyrant' (316). This is a version of the argument made by Peter Boenisch, who turns the traditionally British assertion of the arrogance of the imagined Continental director back on itself. He argues that 'the director who poses as the text or playwright's humble instrument, who considers himself as "simply staging" the text, without taking an interpretive stance, in fact commits the most violent intervention'. That is because this position assumes the right 'to speak for and act on behalf of the "truth of the text" it defines in the first place' (2015, 115). This is auteurism taken to its logical, authoritarian extreme. In asserting their right to speak on behalf of Euripides and his translator, Don Taylor, and in levelling the charge of auteurism at Mitchell, therefore, Billington and Spencer are assuming, in Ahmed's words, 'the right to determine whose wills are willful wills'. An author's will is sovereign; an auteur's is 'overweening arrogance'.

Peter Boenisch (2015, 9) rejects this characterisation of the willful director battling against the playwright in his account of *Regie*, the German term for directing, which he defines as 'a formal operation whereby the play-text remains [. . .] the same, yet our perception and understanding [of it] is ultimately changed'. Boenisch argues that his process 'truly messes up' not 'the authorial privilege of the playwright, but the very order of the sensible, [. . .] in its refusal to "orderly" represent, illustrate and thus to play by the rules of the established hegemonic [. . .] order of things' (186). The term 'order of the sensible' is taken from the philosopher Jacques Rancière (2004). By 'the sensible', Rancière means 'that which can be sensed' (what can be said, heard, seen, felt and thought), or what it is permissible to experience in any given cultural context. He refers to the ordering or 'distribution' of this material to mean how it is organised and disseminated: who is permitted to see it and where and under what circumstances. Rancière proposes that this 'distribution' functions as a 'regime' within which artists and their audiences encounter one another. Therefore, put simply, Boenisch's argument is that, by representing a play-text in unexpected ways, a director may expose and challenge the implicit 'regime' that governs what a culture considers permissible to show, and, by extension, to think.

Although Boenisch does not use the term 'auteur', and with good reason, its appropriation by makers of theatre has often functioned much more like his conception of *Regie* than cinematic auteurism, which is to say that, in the theatre, self-proclaimed 'auteurs' have not generally claimed sole authorship of their work. Prominent among early adopters of the term into the theatre was Roger Planchon, who, as Yvonne Daoust (1981, 17) observed, 'has always integrated cinematic techniques into his *mise en scène* because he regards theatre and film as closely related' (as does Mitchell, of course, whose cinematic influences are well documented, and who almost invariably frames the action of her productions in a cinemascope). Planchon considered that what he called the '*langage scénique*' (the stage language) 'has a responsibility equal to that of the written text', and he therefore believed it was impossible to stage a text without interpretation (Daoust 1981, 15). Planchon's understanding of the responsibility of 'stage language' derived from Brecht, and particularly Brecht's idea of a play's *Fabel*: the sequence of events and interactions that constitute its action. Like Planchon's '*langage scénique*' a *Fabel* is not, however, intended to be a neutral description of the action. Like much of Brecht's thinking, it is dialectical, and therefore seeks to expose contradictions and competing positions within a narrative.

Lucia di Lammermoor

An understanding of dialectical thinking can enable us to see Mitchell's alleged auteurism as something quite different: the creation of a *Fabel* that, in David Barnett's (2015, 86) definition, 'teases out contradictions in order to emphasise them in performance'. Take, for example, her decision to adopt a 'split-screen approach' to staging *Lucia di Lammermoor*.

Here are the responses of three critics. George Hall (2016) in *The Stage*:

> Mitchell's split-screen approach, whereby the audience sees not only the characters meant to be singing at any given moment, but what is happening simultaneously offstage. The effect is hugely *distracting*.
>
> (emphasis added)

Michael Tanner (2016) in *The Spectator*:

> While the main action is on one side, plenty of *distracting* business is being executed on the other, much of it the invention of Mitchell.
>
> (emphasis added)

and Fiona Maddocks (2016) in *The Observer*:

> Attention was drawn constantly to another part of the stage, tearing us from the singer, usually poor Castronovo, who has a powerful, alluring voice but had to battle with compulsive *distractions*.
>
> (emphasis added)

The repeated accusation of 'distraction' is revealing. The verb 'to distract' derives from the Latin *dis-* (away) and *trahere* (to draw). Attention is drawn away, in one or more different directions, from a desired, or intended focus. It brings to mind Ahmed's reading of will as 'the possibility of deviation' (11) and therefore of willfulness as 'the perverse potential of will' and its traces as 'a wayward line' (12). As she writes:

> The willful subject is often depicted as a wanderer. When you stray from official paths, you create desire lines, faint marks on the earth, as traces of where you or others have been.
>
> (21)

Mitchell's critics were right: Distraction was clearly her intention. Her staging was achieved, technically, by a series of 'box sets' that were wheeled into position during scene breaks. These boxes recall the German name for a proscenium auditorium: a *Guckkastenbühne*, literally a 'looking-box-stage'. The proscenium arch creates realistic illusion by presenting a tightly edited collection of objects, images and actions, screened off in order to be looked at. Its space is, therefore, a 'closed, coherent structure', which, as the geographer Doreen Massey (2005, 45, 61) observes, '*cannot exist*' in reality, because space is 'the dimension of dynamic, simultaneous multiplicity'.

If we refuse to accept the illusion of spaces as closed systems, then, we must embrace their constitutively distracting nature. To embrace distraction is to engage with the politics of space, which, as Massey writes, 'presents us with the social in the widest sense: the challenge of our constitutive inter-relatedness, and thus our collective implication in the outcomes of that inter-relatedness' (195). Spaces, in other words, are always composed of relations from which we cannot escape and which exceed any attempt to make them cohere from a single perspective. Mitchell and her designer Vicki Mortimer's split-screen staging of *Lucia* exposed this, by distracting audiences from the opera that, in the critic George Hall's words (2016), they were 'meant to be' seeing.

Donizetti wrote his opera in three acts. The first concludes with a love duet in which Lucia and her lover Edgardo exchange rings. The second reaches its climax with a famous sextet that marks the sudden return of Edgardo (whom Lucia had believed to be unfaithful) during Lucia's arranged marriage. The final act includes Lucia's famous 'mad scene', which follows her off-stage murder of her husband. It concludes, however, not with the death of Lucia (which takes place off stage), but with the suicide of Edgardo. At first sight, this appears to be the plot of a tragic love story. The lovers are briefly united only to be separated and to become the victims of terrible misfortune, with the consequence that Lucia goes mad and dies, and her lover kills himself in grief. But there are contradictions to be teased out. The opera begins with the sighting of an intruder (later revealed to be Edgardo) on Lucia's brother Enrico's property. It ends with Edgardo's suicide, which takes place as he had been waiting for a duel with Enrico, arranged at the start of the third act in what the Metropolitan Opera's synopsis describes as Edgardo's 'dilapidated home'. We might therefore read the whole opera as a duel between Enrico and Edgardo in which not love, but property, is at stake: a story, in other words, about the operations of patriarchy.

Cultural theorist Heidi Hartmann (1979, 11) defined patriarchy as 'a set of social relations between men, which have a material base, and which, though hierarchical, establish and create interdependence and solidarity among men that enable them to dominate women'. To read the opera as an exploration of relations within patriarchy in this way is to follow, for example, Eve Kosofsky Sedgwick's (1985) reading of nineteenth-century literature as structured by male homosocial relations. Mitchell's use of the split stage served initially to expose these relations (in that we saw Enrico's men searching for Edgardo while the main action was elsewhere) and then quickly to expose the ways in which Lucia becomes trapped in relations between men, as Enrico's men searched not only for the intruder but for incriminating evidence in Lucia's private rooms. The split stage served a slightly different function in Act Two, separating Lucia's bedroom stage right, to which men had free access, from her bathroom stage left (to which they did not). Here, Mitchell and Mortimer teased out a further contradiction, this time within the patriarchal structure. We might expect the marriage bed (as the traditional site of both conception and birth) to be placed centrally. But, by offsetting it against the privacy of Lucia's bathroom, Mitchell and Mortimer presented it as a public site, and showed that patriarchy depends, crucially, upon both public and private acceptance. Thus, the bathroom came to stand for the question of women's private willingness to accept their position within patriarchy, which, as Coppélia Kahn (1981, 13) has argued, is 'the invisible heart of the whole structure'. The split stage thus offered a dialectical representation of patriarchal power: Its public domination of women's bodies leaves it vulnerable to their private refusal to accept its terms.

These two uses of the split stage were united in Mitchell's simultaneous staging of the meeting of Enrico and Edgardo at which they agree to duel and Lucia's murder of her husband Arturo, assisted by her maid Alisa. Just as Lucia attempted to escape her enforced marriage by killing her husband, a homosocial contract was established in Enrico and Edgardo's agreement to duel that would make any idea of Lucia's escape from a life governed by male relationships impossible. This reading was consolidated in the staging of Edgardo's dying aria at the opera's close in Lucia's bathroom. Fiona Maddocks (2016) deplored this decision: 'For Castronovo to have to sing his last farewell against the sound of running water was an assault more abominable than any operatic sex or violence', she wrote. But if we read this not as an 'assault', but as a 'distraction' that refuses to allow the male voice to encompass the opera's narrative in its last words, then Mitchell's willfulness, and the distractions that it generates, can be seen as an effective political strategy for exposing the power relations working beneath the surface of the textual narrative.

Fräulein Julie

Mitchell's 2010 production of *Fräulein Julie* for the Schaubühne am Lehniner Platz was, if anything, even more willfully distracting than her *Lucia*. Mitchell approached Strindberg's play, in which an aborted affair between the valet Jean and his master's daughter, Julie, leads to her presumed suicide, as a narrative of the operations of class and gender power. But rather than concentrating on Jean's position as a victim of his class or Julie's confinement by her gender, Mitchell focused on the frequently overlooked housemaid Kristin, whose life is constrained by both of these structural inequalities. Mitchell took the decision to remove anything not experienced by this character. Therefore, as Kristin slept or looked out of the window, or day-dreamed as she washed the dishes, the audience was likewise unaware of allegedly significant plot developments between Jean and Julie, and watched and listened instead to Kristin's dreams, in the form of text excerpted from the Danish poet Inger Christensen's 1981 poem *Alphabet*.

Christensen's poem is structured around the Latin alphabet (its sections begin with successive letters from A to N) and the Fibonacci series (its first section has one line, the next two, then three, five, eight, thirteen and so on). This structure enables the poem to perform a dizzying series of expansive leaps from the plainest of observations (it begins: 'apricot trees exist' (2001, 11) to an ecological perspective on the planet, and back again. These movements are constantly haunted by man's capacity to inflict catastrophe, which lurks at the poem's centre like the poison in an apricot's stone:

> killers exist, and doves, and doves;
> haze, dioxin, and days; days
> exist, days and death; and poems
> exist; poems, days, death (14)

Christensen's poem functioned, in other words, as a willful distraction from the linear dramaturgy of Strindberg's play. It spiralled away from and around the plot, and enabled Mitchell to go much further than merely highlighting the structural violence inflicted on those, such as Kristin, whose voices are silenced in the canon. Its associative leaps from the 'bracken and blackberries' of Kristin's daily perspective to 'bromine [...]; and hydrogen, hydrogen' (12) (foreshadowing the bombs on Hiroshima and Nagasaki) asked what kind of world might be made by a culture that listened to these unheard voices and paid deep attention to the perspectives they might articulate.

The Cherry Orchard

Mitchell's approach to directing canonical works has been consistently both willful and distracting insofar as it has drawn focus away from what audiences expect to see. But she has not always taken such an overtly interventionist approach. Her 2014 production of Chekhov's *The Cherry Orchard* at the Young Vic didn't interpolate either action or text into the play, but nonetheless set out willfully to reject the conventional reading of it, which Mitchell labelled 'gentle introspection around the samovar'. Instead, she promised an 'edgy, fast-moving and frightening' exploration of 'the cruelty and lack of imagination that privilege brings and class ambitions encourage' (Bailey 2014, 97).

This reading was exemplified, for me, in one gesture, which was distracting in that it introduced a set of associations and resonances from Britain in the early twenty-first century rather than Russia just over a century before. The servant Yasha, seducing the maid Dunyasha, suddenly held her at arm's length and assessed her, coldly, before reaching forward, in anticipation of Donald Trump's sickening boast, to grab her. I was distracted not only by shock, but by an anachronistic pun. Yasha is a groom, and, in the language of contemporary Britain, this was grooming. Mitchell's production opened eleven months after the police reported on what seem to have been 450 counts of sexual abuse and rape of girls and women perpetrated by Jimmy Savile (Gray and Watt 2013, 11). It was five and six months respectively after the convictions of Stuart Hall and Rolf Harris for sexual abuse (BBC News 2014a, 2014b). It was two years after the start of Dame Janet Smith's review into incidents of sexual abuse at the BBC and fifteen months before the publication of her final report (Smith 2016). David Mamet (1994, 196) analysed the dramaturgical structure of *The Cherry Orchard* as the same scene played again and again, in which half of a couple attempts 'to consummate, clarify, or rectify an unhappy sexual situation'. This reading can be extended to involve those characters (Pishchik, Firs and Gaev) who Mamet excludes from interest as 'local colour' because they are 'celibate and seen as somewhat doddering in different degrees', if we alter his reading of the subject of these scenes from sex to love. In this version, the play is a series of scenes in which people ask each other 'why don't you love me more?' Mitchell's reading of the play showed us this reiterative pattern but sharpened its repeated, implicit question: 'Why are you hurting me?' her characters asked.

Abuse echoed everywhere in this production. For example, Mitchell moved Act Two indoors. This decision fitted her preference for sets that represent bounded spaces, but it also meant that the empty bed of Ranevskaya's drowned son remained upstage almost throughout, haunting the action with its silent reproach. Angus Wright's Gaev also strongly rejected the conventional characterisation of studied, nonchalant denial and aristocratic absent-mindedness. Wright created instead a portrait of extreme anxiety, punctuated by sharp tics that spoke of buried trauma. Dominic Rowan's Lopakhin likewise resisted the traditional bourgeois reading of the role of peasant-turned-businessman as a kindly but rational man whose only choice is to buy Ranevskaya's estate and make it profitable. He began by making rational arguments, but by the end his decisions were transparently vindictive and vengeful: punishing Ranevskaya's cruel treatment of him in childhood, the scars of which clearly had not healed.

Reviewing representations of child sexual abuse in recent British theatre in 2013, Anna Harpin (2013, 181) demonstrated conclusively that treatments of the subject have been characterised, almost unanimously, by 'a seemingly unremarkable heterosexism' that works to underwrite 'misperceptions about child sexual abuse' and to 'shore up established fictions of gender and sexual practices'. By contrast, Mitchell's *Cherry Orchard* used productively distracting contemporary references to challenge the assumption that abuse is a grotesque anomaly rather than a common feature of lived experience. By following the traces of these willful distractions from the play's apparent subject, it was possible to read in the production what the reports of the inquiries led by Dame Janet Smith and Sir William Macpherson (1999) have shown: that abuse is, by its very nature, systemic and is produced by structural inequality. Thus, as Mitchell's production closed with the text's violent uprooting of the cherry orchard and the collapse of the forgotten servant Firs in the abandoned house, it was impossible not to experience these actions as instances of abuse, and to reflect that abusive behaviour does not go against the grain of social history. Mitchell proposed that abuse is that grain and that it can be read as clearly as the rings of a tree.

Distraction and Affinity

In all three of these productions, therefore, we can see Mitchell's allegedly 'misguided' thoughts and 'distracting' effects as political strategies to resist the hegemonic values that are routinely asserted by canonical texts and which underwrite their canonical status. She uses distraction willfully to expose operations and abuses of power, and to redirect the audience's attention to characters and experiences that are commonly overlooked. But Sara Ahmed (2014, 167) warns that willfulness can also distract us from recognising the privilege of our own position: 'the very assumption of willfulness', she writes, 'can protect some from realizing how their goals are already accomplished by the general will'. The experience of battling willfully against authority in one area can blind us to the ways in which we may, from other perspectives, be more closely aligned with it than we may be willing or able to see. Mitchell (2009, 3–4) makes a similar argument in her book *The Director's Craft*, where she counsels directors to be aware of 'affinities': 'things that you are drawn to in the play because they relate to your own life or how you look at the world'. These, Mitchell warns, 'can be both useful and somewhat limiting' because they give you 'special insight' but 'could stop you seeing other aspects of the play'. The productions that I have analysed show Mitchell using affinity creatively, by distracting audiences from what they may be instinctively drawn to, and thereby exposing the relations of power that influence how we look at the world.

It is important to note, in concluding, however, that Mitchell's project is not without its unspoken affinities. You may, for example, have noticed in the images illustrating these talks online that her casting has not been ethnically diverse, a fact that is rarely remarked upon in public discussions of her work, but is unmistakable once noticed.[1] It's important to say, by way of mitigation, that Mitchell often works with permanent ensembles in European theatres, whose performers are usually entirely or overwhelmingly white, and she does not, therefore, have the freedom to cast anyone she chooses. But she has also worked with what Rebellato (2010, 328) has described as 'a kind of informal repertory company' in her UK productions who are also exclusively white. In her advice for directors on casting, Mitchell (2009, 102) notes the importance of 'how [actors] will fit into a group of people who need to work together', and clearly the relationships that have developed among members of her informal ensemble are likely to generate a positive group dynamic.

But Mitchell's project to expose political realities that are commonly overlooked should alert us to the problematic exclusion of actors of colour from British stages today just as it enables us to see the exclusion of women (and working-class women in particular) from canonical texts. Racial prejudice may not be the subject of her work, but ethnicity is legible in it nonetheless, and may prompt us to question whether the act of staging plays from white cultures with white casts in diverse European cities today may unintentionally participate in the continuing white-washing of history that actively excludes people of colour from cultural narratives in which they (like Lucia, and the maids Kristin and Dunyasha) also have a stake.[2] Mitchell's political agenda seems to have distracted her from these challenging questions surrounding the representation of ethnic identities in particular. But her strategy of willful distraction from the agenda of canonical authority in relation to gender and class does offer a model of intervention that might be usefully applied to other forms of systemic exclusion, that she has, until now, overlooked.

Productions

Women of Troy (2007), National Theatre (Lyttelton), London
Fräulein Julie (2010), Schaubühne am Lehniner Platz, Berlin

The Cherry Orchard (2014), Young Vic, London
Lucia di Lammermoor (2016), Royal Opera House, London

Notes

1 A notable exception is the actor and campaigner Danny Lee Wynter, who tweeted, for example, about Mitchell's production of Sarah Kane's *Cleansed*: 'Zero critics reviewing Katie Mitchell's *Cleansed* call out her prolific on-stage racism. Probably cos they're all white too & don't notice!' (@dannyleewynter, 10.10am, 24 February 2016).
2 I chose in the recorded lecture to use the term 'race' rather than 'ethnicity' in this section in the spirit of W.J.T. Mitchell (2012), who argues that race is paradoxically both non-existent and a means by which our vision of the world is mediated. I have decided, however, to revise my terminology for this published version and use the term 'ethnicity' instead. This is because 'ethnicity' can refer, intersectionally, to multiple identities and incorporates cultural aspects of identity (such as nationality), whereas the term 'race' is assumed (inaccurately) to be biological and unitary.

References

Ahmed, Sara (2014). *Willful Subjects*. Durham, NC: Duke University Press.

Bailey, Kate (2014). 'Avant-Garde and Actuality: Interviews with Stage Director Katie Mitchell and Set Designer Vicki Mortimer', in *Russian Avant-Garde Theatre: War, Revolution and Design*, ed. John E. Bowlt. London: Nick Hern Books. 92–103.

Barnett, David (2015). *Brecht in Practice: Theatre, Theory and Performance*. London: Bloomsbury.

BBC News (2014a). 'Stuart Hall Sentenced for Indecent Assaults', 23 May, www.bbc.co.uk/news/uk-england-27540137, accessed on 16 June 2107.

BBC News (2014b). 'Rolf Harris Jailed for Five Years and Nine Months', 4 July, www.bbc.co.uk/news/uk-28163593, accessed on 16 June 2017.

BBC News (2016). 'Royal Opera House Audience Boo Violent Production of Lucia di Lammermoor', 8 April, www.bbc.co.uk/news/entertainment-arts-35995554, accessed on 16 June 2017.

Billington, Michael (2007). 'Review: Women of Troy', *The Guardian*, 29 November, www.theguardian.com/stage/2007/nov/29/theatre.euripides, accessed on 13 June 2017.

Billington, Michael (2009). 'Don't Let Auteurs Take Over in Theatre', 14 April, www.theguardian.com/stage/theatreblog/2009/apr/14/auteur-theatre, accessed on 13 June 2017.

Boenisch, Peter (2015). *Directing Scenes and Senses: The Thinking of Regie*. Manchester: Manchester University Press.

Christensen, Inger, trans. Susanna Nied (2001). *Alphabet*. New York: New Directions.

Christiansen, Rupert (2016). 'Lucia di Lammermoor, Royal Opera, Verdict: Too Leaden Even for the Hecklers', *The Daily Telegraph*, 8 April, www.telegraph.co.uk/opera/what-to-see/lucia-di-lammermoor-royal-opera-house-verdict-too-leaden-even-fo/, accessed on 16 June 2017.

Daoust, Yvonne (1981). *Roger Planchon: Director and Playwright*. Cambridge: Cambridge University Press.

Gray, David, and Peter Watt (2013). 'Giving Victims a Voice: Joint Report into Sexual Allegations Made against Jimmy Savile', *Metropolitan Police and the National Society for the Prevention of Cruelty to Children*, January, www.nspcc.org.uk/globalassets/documents/research-reports/yewtree-report-giving-victims-voice-jimmy-savile.pdf, accessed on 16 June 2017.

Hall, George (2016). 'Katie Mitchell directs Lucia Di Lammermoor review at the Royal Opera House, London', *The Stage*, 7 April, www.thestage.co.uk/reviews/2016/lucia-di-lammermoor-review-at-the-royal-opera-house-london/, accessed on 16 June 2017.

Harpin, Anna (2013). 'Unremarkable Violence: Staging Child Sexual Abuse in Recent British Theatre', *Contemporary Theatre Review* 23.2: 166–181.

Hartmann, Heidi (1979). 'The Unhappy Marriage of Marxism and Feminism: Towards a More Progressive Union', *Capital & Class* 3. DOI:10.1177/030981687900800102.

Kahn, Coppélia (1981). *Man's Estate: Masculine Identity in Shakespeare.* Oakland, CA: University of California Press.

Kosofsky Sedgwick, Eve (1985). *Between Men: English Literature and Male Homosocial Desire.* New York: Columbia University Press.

MacPherson, William (1999). 'The Stephen Lawrence Inquiry', February, www.gov.uk/government/uploads/system/uploads/attachment_data/file/277111/4262.pdf, accessed on 16 June 2017.

Maddocks, Fiona (2016). 'Lucia di Lammermoor Review – Flawed but Full of Provocative Thought', *The Observer*, 10 April, www.theguardian.com/music/2016/apr/10/lucia-di-lammermoor-review-royal-opera-katie-mitchell-diana-damrau, accessed on 16 June 2017.

Mamet, David (1994). *A Whore's Profession: Notes and Essays.* London: Faber and Faber.

Massey, Doreen (2005). *For Space.* London: Sage Publications.

Metropolitan Opera (undated). 'Synopsis: Lucia di Lammermoor', www.metopera.org/discover/synposes-archive/lucia-di-lammermoor/, accessed on 16 June 2017.

Mitchell, Katie (2009). *The Director's Craft: A Handbook for the Theatre.* Abingdon: Routledge.

Mitchell, William John Thomas (2012). *Seeing Through Race.* Cambridge, MA: Harvard University Press.

Rancière, Jacques, trans. Gabriel Rockhill (2004). *The Politics of Aesthetics: The Distribution of the Sensible.* London: Continuum.

Rebellato, Dan (2010). 'Katie Mitchell: Learning from Europe', in *Contemporary European Theatre Directors*, ed. Maria Delgado and Dan Rebellato. Abingdon: Routledge. 317–338.

Royal Opera House (2016). 'Important information about the Royal Opera's Lucia di Lammermoor', email to author, 14 March, 12.44pm.

Spencer, Charles (2007). 'Women of Troy: Euripides All Roughed Up', *The Daily Telegraph*, 30 November, www.telegraph.co.uk/culture/theatre/drama/3669609/Women-of-Troy-Euripides-all-roughed-up.html, accessed on 16 June 2017.

Smith, Dame Janet (2016). 'The Dame Janet Smith Review Report: An Independent Review into the BBC's Culture and Practices during the Jimmy Saviel and Stuart Hall Years', 25 February, http://downloads.bbci.co.uk/bbctrust/assets/files/pdf/our_work/dame_janet_smith_review/conclusions_summaries.pdf, accessed on 16 June 2017.

Tanner, Michael (2016). 'Tame and Drowning in Detail: Royal Opera's Lucia di Lammermoor Reviewed', *The Spectator*, 16 April, www.spectator.co.uk/2016/04/tame-and-drowning-in-detail-royal-operas-lucia-di-lammermoor-reviewed/, accessed on 16 June 2017.

4

Stages and screens

Katie Mitchell's theatre aesthetics

Leo Warner in conversation with Janis Jefferies

Edited transcript of conversation | 7th July 2017 | Lyric Hammersmith, London
Link | digitaltheatreplus.com/4x45/katiemitchell/stagesand screens

JANIS JEFFERIES: I'm Janis Jefferies from Goldsmiths College, London, and I'm really delighted to be in conversation with Leo Warner. I'm going to introduce myself and let Leo introduce himself, just so we can set the scene a little bit. I'm actually from a visual arts background. My passion for Katie Mitchell and the impact of all sorts of technology on contemporary theatre and performance started in the 1970s when I studied at the Poznań Academy of Arts in Poland with the sculptor Magdalena Abakanowicz, who was a contemporary of the Polish theatre director Jerzy Grotowski and very influenced by him. It was normal practice to work with poor materials, props and installations in different environments. I had opportunities to go and see theatre in Poland which I had never seen the likes of in Britain, such as Józef Szajna's underground theatre in Warsaw, Tadeusz Kantor's production of

The Dead Class in Kraków (1975), and Grotowski's work in Wrocław. This was very much a period of experimentation, of working with objects and sounds, and breaking traditions and boundaries between painting and sculpture. When I came back to England after this experience, it took many years before I saw someone like Katie Mitchell, who seemed to me to challenge the dominant literary conventions of theatre in this country. I first saw Mitchell's wonderful production of Chekhov's *The Seagull* at the National Theatre, London, in 2006, where actors rushed around the stage in a frenzy; objects, like plates, were smashed and a stuffed seagull was thrown wall-to-wall in an enclosed interior, a bit like a Pina Bausch performance, and I was completely addicted.

We're going to talk about the impact of Katie Mitchell's work on British theatre, and on Leo, yourself, in terms of the work you've done with her over the years, but perhaps you'd like to introduce yourself first, so people know who you are.

LEO WARNER: Certainly. I am the founder, and one of the directors, of a company called 59 Productions and I'm from a graphic design background originally. I studied English at the University of York and set the company up – fifteen years ago now – as a way to continue to work and develop collaborative relationships with a number of specific individuals, some of whom I'm still working with, and many others who have since come on board. The company has broadened its remit far and wide, and I suppose you could say insofar as we have a specialty it's design-based. We are particularly interested in working with new technologies, and specifically video, but we've recently continued to expand the company to include architects, writers, musicians and so on, and there is now in the region of thirty of us, full time, with offices in London and New York. The work that we have done over those fifteen years started very much on the page and on the screen, then came into the world of the stage, theatre in particular, before branching out into opera and ballet and other live art forms. We then went on to work in ceremonies and events and exhibitions and, more recently, public artwork. So it's a very broad world that I work in, but I first worked with Katie on *Waves* in 2006, which was the first show that we worked on at all at the National Theatre and has proved, I think it's fair to say, and as you point out, a huge influence on me over the years.

JJ: I went five times to that particular production. I thought Virginia Woolf's novel *The Waves* was unperformable, and unfilmable. It is such a work of imaginative fiction that it puts images in your head, and you have an intimacy with characters that seems difficult to translate to the stage. The reason why I went five times is because I sat at the back, I sat in the middle, I sat at the side, I sat at the front, partly because I'd never seen anything comparable in the way that the technology and the screen worked together with such intensity. So I'm really interested to know what happened in the rehearsal room to bring you to use the screen and the props in that way, and the kinds of contributions you thought you were being challenged to think about in the rehearsal room.

LW: Yes, well, I suppose it was a very organic process on account of us being very much thrown in at the deep end and, in fact, the reason it came about was that we'd just done a bit of video design work for a show called

Black Watch (2006), which was produced by the National
Theatre of Scotland, and actually it was almost a cold call
to the National Theatre; we knew some people and just
said, 'We've just done this show, it would be great to have
a conversation', and within two or three days, I think, we
had a meeting with the Head of Production, and within
a week I was in a rehearsal room working with Katie.
She'd already done some experimentation in a workshop
with cameras and had convinced herself and, indeed,
the National Theatre, that an approach to this apparently unadaptable, unstageable literary source text was to
use cameras to somehow bridge the divide between the
words and something that might be termed a dramatic,
or theatrical, experience. So there was no time to make a
plan or discuss it, and I think they'd even done a week's
rehearsal before I joined them, doing some very early
experiments with handicams and things. I suppose I just
did the only thing I knew how, which was to start framing shots, almost in the most banal sense of, 'What is the
detail we want to see here?' and with a burning interest in
aesthetic form, and therefore proportion and design – the
design of a shot; that was how I approached it. It was very
much a sort of aesthetic-led approach. I knew the novel
from university, but I really didn't know Katie's work
particularly. We just started making shots and they started
adding up, and over the course of the seven- or eight-
week rehearsal period, we built what I suppose were a
series of vignettes, really delivered to examine each of the
main characters individually, over several periods of their
lives. So they were glimpses and vignettes, and because
they were self-contained in that way, we could make it
in a very modular way, which was the only thing which

made it possible, because our later work, as you know, becomes much more feature film-like, and it's sort of continuous.

JJ: It's more cinematic.

LW: Yes, exactly. Yes, and the nature of the work in the rehearsal room was, I suppose, improvisational, in the sense that it was devising. There was as much work going on dramaturgically, in terms of picking out literary fragments from the source text, by Katie, but also by members of the acting company, and the development we were doing in sound – you know, she worked very extensively with Gareth Fry, the amazing sound designer, who we continue to work with – but it was all happening there and Katie is famed, notorious for having huge levels of technical support in the rehearsal room as well as in the theatre, and so we had quite a lot of stuff there, although I have to say nowhere near the same kind of technical support we now have on our productions, which is essentially a full technical rehearsal throughout the rehearsal period. This is a bit more like the world you might experience in those really big sorts of cirque-style shows, where they do 'creation', which involves everyone being in a room for six months.

JJ: It always struck me that perhaps in the rehearsal room it's more like a sort of studio laboratory.

LW: Yes, very much so.

JJ: I am struck by how Mitchell has a very particular sense of what she wants. As a director, she has a very distinctive take on Naturalism, some might say an 'extreme' Naturalism, a stripped down understanding of Stanislavski's Naturalism that makes actors perform as though they were like a machine. Paradoxically, the more the actors' movements are studied and the text is stripped away, there is an emotional rawness to the detail of how somebody might think through a particular physical action and how that thought and action gets visualised. However, there is also a very strong visual aesthetic in this work, combined with an intense rehearsal process in the studio laboratory, which pulls the viewer into the work when seen on stage.

LW: Yes. It's interesting, because I think Katie and I, for whatever reason, share quite a lot in the way of aesthetic taste, including our formal interest in shot structure and indeed narrative structure, actually, which of course in her case is very heavily influenced by Eastern European traditions – you mentioned Pina Bausch, and Russian directors as well. That aesthetic world is something which I'm very interested in too, especially from a graphic point of view. But it's interesting that you mentioned the words 'laboratory environment', which is how it feels. It's also incredibly tightly controlled and the way the room is run is extremely precise, as you would expect.

JJ: I would imagine it was extremely precise, because I saw, for example, . . . *some trace of her* (National Theatre, London 2008). We might just touch on the complexity of an actor having to be the performer, change character, having to be a Foley artist – it seems to me to be an extraordinary thing, how tight the choreographic marks are on the floor. So, even if it's kind of experimental, it's also very tight in the way it's formally constructed.

LW: Yes, I mean, the complexity of those shows, and the limitations in terms of time and money, are such that it has to be incredibly efficient; we really can't afford to throw away more than a couple of minutes a day, because you might make one shot in that time, but in a show which is built of four, five or six hundred shots, that's all you can do; just keep making the individual components that build this significant piece. And when we started with *Waves*, of course, we had no idea what it was going to take us to devise these individual moments. You know, we ran into real trouble in the early previews because we simply couldn't string it together. We'd made it in fragments, but putting it together was almost impossible.

JJ: I remember that, because it was stated that it had an indefinite running time, so basically it might be longer or shorter, depending on how you could edit on the fly, how long the pauses were.

LW: Yes, I mean, once we'd finished it, it was a fairly definitive length, to within a few minutes. But certainly when we started on stage, we just had no idea of the technical complexity of taking it from the rehearsal room into the theatre. We now know, and we now plan for that extremely well, but yes, at the time it was an unknown quantity.

JJ: How do you move from rehearsal on to the stage, given that laboratory environment? It would be very helpful to know the different contributions people make. Mitchell is a director, I would say, in an Eastern European sense – the *machine* is the text; it's not about being somehow controlled by the intentions of the author, which seems to upset a lot of people here in England, but it is a particular vision. So, how does that get moved on to the stage? Given that the machine is like a text, and the performers are also machinic in some ways.

LW: Yes. I'm afraid the answer to that is rather banal, which is we try and replicate the machine as thoroughly as possible in the rehearsal room, to the point where really our ideal process would be to work on the stage that we will be ultimately putting the piece on to, but we more or less now run the tech as a transfer; it's almost like we complete as much as we possibly can in the rehearsal room, and then we just simply remove it and install it into the theatre.

JJ: Right, so you go from one space to another.

LW: That's from a technical point of view. Actually, the way these things run is we tend to . . . Obviously we can't string everything together until the very final stages of rehearsal, and at that point, we quite often make quite big changes, so we will then hit the stage with a pretty significant list of things we actually do want to alter, and they tend to be dramaturgical decisions.

JJ: Can you give an example?

LW: Yes, we quite often add scenes at the very beginning or the very end; like, completely new scenes that we haven't previously conceived. Framing devices, I suppose. Once we know what the piece is, we can see that we need to therefore manage, or at least set, expectations in a particular way to give people a basis on which to engage with the main body of the piece. So, quite a lot of those opening sequences – in *The Forbidden Zone* (2014), for example, which I know you've seen. . .

JJ: Yes, I saw that twice.

LW: Very good. We were going to start it, I think, on the train, but we decided to build a sequence with the main character on the platform, waiting for the train, and building in an interaction with another character that sets up the events that happen in what is essentially the first scene. It tends to be a way of explaining the language of the machine to people, so they can see the components, understand how the piece is being made, and then choose whether to continue to watch the construction process, or whether to watch what we call the final output, which is the cinematic element.

JJ: I think that's very interesting, because when you're in, particularly Poland, actually, there is a whole kind of structuralist history of certain kinds of practices, whether that's in architecture or sculpture, and it is about revealing that component or that module. In a way, I suppose, what you're suggesting is that it is setting the scene.

LW: Yes.

JJ: Because there isn't linear time, history isn't running as a thread. It's quite – I would say – a fractured narrative, if we think in terms of English literature, which is why, I suppose, Mitchell showed that passion for Virginia Woolf. It is in fragments because life isn't lived as a continuous line.

LW: Yes.

JJ: It's fragmentary and yet you have to somehow hold something coherently for, perhaps, audiences who are used to a beginning, middle and end in a particular form.

LW: Yes. I mean, some of the pieces are fairly linear, but I think it's fair to say that I don't think there's a single one which doesn't have what we might call another ingredient, or another element, which is quite often something that stylistically cuts across the main narrative if there is one – I mean, there always is one – which is either a dream, or a memory or a history.

JJ: They're like little nuggets, aren't they? Because there isn't a lot of change of scenes and actions, like you talked about in *The Forbidden Zone* just now, but sometimes there are things staged next to one another. Or in the opera *Written on Skin* (2012), you've got different elements, again, of a module construction, concurrently.

LW: Yes, and I think both Katie and I are interested in this idea that, as you say, we don't experience our lives in a consistent linear way. There's a fragmentary nature to existence and experience, and that is something which I think the medium that we've kind of created, by picking elements from lots of different forms, celebrates – that fragmentation and that difference of the subjectivity of experience.

JJ: Yes. As somebody who sits in these different positions in the theatre, I think it's quite extraordinary how sucked in you become to minute details or actions, whether it's the movement on the stage or, indeed, how the technology is working. They don't seem to be merely illustrative, they're not naturalistic; any illusion you might have is denied. You know you're watching something very particularly constructed.

LW: Yes.

JJ: And that's a very conscious, formal scenario, from the rehearsal room again?

LW: Yes, absolutely, and I suppose it's partly about how we made the work; the fragmentary nature of the construction somehow, when it works well – and I think *Waves* is a really good example of that – is a sort of mirror image of the fragmentary nature of the material. It works best when you have something which celebrates the subjectivity of experience, as Virginia Woolf does in that amazing novel, because you can see that the different stimuli (sound, image, music, physicality) are all being constructed literally in different parts of the stage. To an extent, by filming them and miking people, and mixing the sound, and mixing music in and everything, we are linearising it to a point, but you can still, as a member of the audience, look anywhere on stage and see how that element is being constructed. In fact, just to pick another example, *Wunschkonzert* (2008) – the Franz Xaver Kroetz play that we did in Cologne originally – essentially follows the final hours of a woman who commits suicide, and that woman, who we sort of forensically examined for the hour and a quarter, is constructed from multiple actors – two, in fact. One who plays the face and body and does all the wide shots, and another who does the hands. So any time you cut to a close-up of her doing something, it's a different woman from the one whose face we can see.

JJ: So you see that completely fabricated?

LW: You can see that right there on stage; you can see the woman in the completely naturalistic detailed film set of her apartment, and entirely separately from that, you can see the woman who is mimicking all of the actions which involve her hands on a table which is completely devoid of any additional dressing beyond what's in the frame of the camera. So, building a character from multiple performers is also really fascinating, because that's also, I think, a little bit about how we experience life ourselves, being not quite as straightforward as linear individual storytelling might represent it.

JJ: Yes, Józef Szajna used to do that, sometimes, in the 1970s in the theatre in Warsaw. So you'd have one person coming and doing something, and then another, and it was entirely as a constructivist installation, or sculpture. People use different terms, but it wasn't that somehow it was the actor performing; it was articulating something about an interior life.

LW: Yes, specific.

JJ: Or then it was about the Cold War and things that couldn't be said, so they had to find ways, means, gestures and props to somehow express some kind of inner emotion.

LW: Well, I think one of the things that is quite interesting about the hand example is that it was almost dictated by the technical limitations of the form, because we wanted to be able to get extreme close-ups; we work quite often in extreme detail, but we weren't able to get enough cameras into the what we call 'film sets', in order to be able to cut from a wide-shot into an extreme close-up without doing it from a very long way away. So we formulated this idea that, through continuity of action, you could build the illusion when you cut the piece together so that when someone reaches out to get a glass of water – because of the language we understand, because we've been conditioned through film – when you cut to a close-up of a hand picking up a glass of water, so long as you haven't done anything like crossing the line, your brain just believes it's one and the same.

JJ: Oh yes, perceptually you put the two together, that's how you create the fusion.

LW: Yes, and sometimes we can use that to actually cut against expectation as well, so there are inconsistencies as well as consistencies in how we edit things together. And, of course, there's the element of chance, so when things sometimes are not entirely in sync, you get a jolt, or a jump, which you don't necessarily fully understand, but sort of re-heightens your awareness of the action occasionally.

JJ: It's a kind of glitch, isn't it, which makes you sometimes think, 'Oh, I wonder if that quite worked'.

LW: Yes, it reminds you that you're there. It reminds you that it's live.

Can I ask *you* a question? I know it's been a continuum over a period of ten years of developing this work, but how would you describe one of these shows to someone who didn't know it? One of these, what Katie calls, 'multimedia shows'.

JJ: Well, I think of it as something which is entirely hybrid, which is radicalising a very conventional culture that, in my view, depends on certain literary theatrical traditions; which is really trying to get inside a character, often and mostly women, which is the other great joy – seeing so many women on the stage performing; which tells particular stories about people's lives, like in *The Forbidden Zone*, those two characters coming together, the words being spoken, drawing on so many different interconnected relationships that are then revealed. So I might describe it as a completely physical sensory experience, but you're not in physical theatre, and you're not in conventional literary theatre, but you are absolutely going to be spellbound, drained, and images haunt you much later. I mean, you get it with some novels, I'm sure. You, I know, have just directed *City of Glass* (2017), and there is something about Paul Auster's writing that's very visual. Images carry with you, and I think the best of Mitchell that I've seen in London, dare I say, they stay with you, they haunt you. It's a bit like the idea of a kind of after-effect, an after-impact. But I have also taken friends who have wondered what all the fuss is about.

LW: What's going on, yes.

JJ: Because it isn't cinema, it's not theatre. If you're a strict, strict, in-the-box person, then you are confused, but

I defy anyone not to have their hair stand on the skin, just to be mesmerised by, you know, some of the images from *Waves*, where Neville's looking through a pane of glass. The camera, operated by another performer, focuses on the face behind the glass, an image projected onto the screen. A woman gazes through a window on a rainy day. You hear the sound of rain falling on the pane but you also see faces in close-up and the muscles of the performers twinging. It just gives you a whole different kind of synthesis between inside and outside worlds.

LW: Wonderful. What a write-up!

JJ: But this isn't about me; this is about how you began to work. You mentioned Cologne; sadly I have never travelled to France or Germany, and it is a great sadness that there was quite a period where you couldn't see a Katie Mitchell production in England. I appreciate that the input and the technologies for this kind of work are expensive, but it seems as though there is much more recognition for it in mainland Europe than there is here. Would you think that's a fair comment? And for you, working in Germany, let's say, as opposed to one of our national theatres – have you noticed a shift, or a change in the dynamic, in the way of working, or the audience to the work?

LW: Yes. I mean, there's no doubt that it became very difficult for us to do this specific type of work certainly in London, and actually London was really the only place in the UK at that time where the theatres were substantial enough to support the budgets for something which is inherently, I think, to an extent an acquired taste. You talk about bringing friends to see Katie Mitchell shows, and them not understanding why you would want to make a piece of theatre like that. It happens instinctively for me that I am interested in that, and I'm not particularly interested in what you might call standard form, whatever that is, because I don't particularly know what that is, and therefore I'm very happy to absorb this sort of narrative in whatever collection of stimuli someone wants to play with. But, yes, there's no doubt that the critical response to this experiment in particular, I think, which started with *Waves* and then went on with *Attempts on Her Life* (2007) . . .

JJ: Yes, the Martin Crimp play.

LW: And then shortly thereafter we experimented with opera, we did a version of [Henry Purcell's] *Dido and Aeneas* called *After Dido* with English National Opera and the Young Vic (2009), and there was a real sense, because we were exploring a form – and actually, I feel fairly strongly, developing it quite rapidly – that people very quickly started to say, 'We've seen this before', critically. 'We've seen this before, is this the only idea that she has? Why are we still looking at video cameras and screens on stage?' – which I struggled with at the time, being confused by the problem that you might make a body of work that does drill into something which is kind of fascinating, both from a technical and a creative point of view. Why not explore it and continue to explore it for as long as it remains alive and active? And it was very aggressive, interestingly – people took our work quite personally, and it became quite difficult to get the work made, and for various reasons we were offered the opportunity to explore it, in particular in Germany to begin with, and we took it.

Whether audiences relate differently to it? I think there is a much less set sense, where I've worked in Germany at least, that theatre should be a particular way. That's not to say there aren't huge swathes of people in the UK who are very happy to absorb theatre in whatever form it's offered to them. But when you come into what might be called the mainstream (and I think the National Theatre needs, to a great extent, to serve large numbers of people in order to deliver on its business model), there was a real sense that this couldn't really exist in that world, and that we had to therefore look elsewhere for the opportunities. And audiences sort of didn't bat an eyelid, to be honest, when we started opening work of this variety in Berlin, or Cologne and beyond. We just felt very much like they were judging it on the basis of the quality, and the intellectual rigour, and the aesthetic standards, but not repeatedly asking the question, 'Is this theatre?' which, I have to say, got a bit boring.

JJ: I understand that from when I had my own experiences in Eastern Europe. Art and theatre were completely experimental, and I had never experienced anything like it before. Mitchell saw Tadeusz Kantor's work when she studied directing in Europe. I also saw Kantor's productions. It seemed strange and foreign at the time but the use of props and actors focusing on physical action and the raw power of their emotions was really powerful. It undid what I understood to be the conventions of theatre and directing.

I think it's interesting that you said that it's a bit like, 'What's new?' and you might want to say, 'Well, actually, I'm exploring something very particularly', in something that you're forming which is shifting a culture. I mean, you could say that Virginia Woolf wrote the same novel nine times if you're going to be that way inclined. But the kind of depth of saying, 'How does this work?' – which is the sort of engineer's question, I always think. You know, how do you tackle this? I've mostly seen things in Poland and Russia, where it is perfectly acceptable. It's almost like, as a director, you don't have to be faithful to anything; you can direct. And I suppose people call that an 'auteur' approach, which is something that maybe in this country is uncomfortable for some?

LW: Yes. I mean, I have to admit I've never fully understood the nature of the criticism.

JJ: The work itself also, I think, is not staged to be nostalgic or comfortable, or romantic. You know, it treats an audience with intelligence; it's challenging. You can feel you're spying; you're kind of undone by certain things. You can't just sort of slob about in a seat.

LW: No, I'd say Katie's been one of the most consistent directors I know, in the sense that her work is a continued exploration of some very tightly defined themes, and in particular the forensic examination of grief, which I think is fascinating, because it's such an extraordinary collection of emotions, and is therefore so dramatically and emotionally rich. I find that really compelling, not just in the work we've done together, but watching her work which I've had no involvement in whatsoever. The creation of this medium, if that's what it is, this art form, is really just an extension of that. It's an opportunity. What the cameras gave Katie was an opportunity to get even closer to everything, but in particular to the actors and their faces, and their actions.

JJ: And it never feels like you are being a voyeur. When I use the word 'spying' it's like you're being invited to share in a moment, but also to release something to reflect upon yourself.

LW: That's interesting.

JJ: I think it's interesting you mentioned grief because, for me, there's a slightly melancholic edge to this work, which I think is also very Eastern European; a kind of melancholia of reflection, particularly in relation to history and time. And it's not that somehow we have to go back to make an easy story, but how do we think about what we do in the future in relation to those fragments of knowledge? Which is why I think it's interesting that you used the word grief there.

LW: I think it's really fundamental to her oeuvre. Insofar as it's possible to plot connections between her pieces of work, that's a very strong through line, and it's something which I'm personally very fascinated by as well, so that connection is, I think, critical in the way that we both address it. I can visually get her closer, and what she can do is to elicit those performances.

JJ: The grief and melancholia – it comes out because there's often a feel of a very dark, murky interior, a sort of nineteenth-century mood, I would call it. And there's Mitchell's interest in Francesca Woodman, who's an extraordinary American photographer active in the 1970s, who creates images of the woman sort of pressed inside. There's a sense of melancholia or grieving in how you use photography, or those moments where you've researched some kind of very particular visual aesthetic, to reinforce the very raw moments of an interior life silently but violently exploding on stage in forensic detail.

LW: Yes, I have to say that the darkness factor is partly a shared taste thing, as well. Interestingly, it also has a quite boring technical aspect to it, which is that the more brightly you light a scene, the sharper the image becomes, and the more you become aware of the digital nature of the technology. If you were shooting for film . . . you know, I'm a terrible director of photography, because I light way too dark for things, and then it's impossible to grade the image up. But because we're shooting for live, and we're only doing a limited amount of grading on the fly (in fact, it's all pre-programmed, so there's no live grading happening; it's happening in a pre-programmed system), we light more or less naturalistically, and that means that we're mimicking real light sources. In the case of a lot of the environments that we're building, they're interiors for obvious reasons. Well, maybe not obvious; I should say that we make them interior because it's easier than doing exterior.

JJ: Intensity; it's also very intense, isn't it, the focus?

LW: Yes, it tends to be about people in their private spaces, or in very tight spaces, and so there is actually the fairly practical thing that to light brightly gives away, to some extent, some of the technology which we're less interested in seeing; but there are, you know, great moments of release when you do suddenly go into a daylight scene, and you realise that we can do that, but we just choose not to for large swathes of the production.

JJ: And there's something maybe with water too. . .

LW: There's quite a lot with water, yes. Getting nature in there, actually, either through light, or through the elements, in the old-fashioned sense of the word, is also fairly fundamental. And I think that's very heavily influenced by people like Francesca Woodman, and this sense of creeping nature, that things are sort of penetrating the human-built world that are slightly uncontrollable, or at least organic.

JJ: Which is interesting when you've had to build and stage constructively these elements. So there are quite a lot of paradoxes.

LW: Yes, getting nature into something which is incredibly tightly formed and technically complex is tricky.

JJ: So, how, over these productions – because you've worked on several now, here and abroad, and in opera as well – how have you dealt with the challenges of technology, which is moving so fast? How have you kind of curtailed it, or kept abreast of the developments, doing the work, and pre-programming on the fly, without it overwhelming the sense of the piece itself? It seems it's very difficult. I mean, by the time you get to *The Forbidden Zone* it's extraordinarily complex.

LW: Yes, I mean, technology isn't moving quite as fast as I would like, to be honest.

JJ: Oh, really? How so?

LW: The fact that we're still not really able to use wireless cameras is maddening. But, having said that, one of the things that you described earlier, about the machine of the piece, the chorography of the stage is, again, largely dictated by camera cable management; and it's maddening, in a way, but in a way it's part of the beauty of it. There was a moment in *Waves* when we were doing a series of close-up shots along a very, very long table, and there were two camera operators and they were sort of leap-frogging each other, which basically means that the camera cables get tangled. At the end of that sequence – it's a brilliant sequence – the two actors who are operating cameras just have to walk round and round each other and then separate, and if they get the turns right the cables then peel off in the middle and you carry on.

That's one of my favourite bits of the show, and there's nothing else to look at.

JJ: How do you actually find those performers? You work with very particular people who must feel confident that, as a performer, they can suddenly work with a camera. That transition is not easy; not many can do it.

LW: Yes, I mean, not always. No, it's incredibly difficult. No, and we end up with productions where we discover an actor is particularly adept at using a camera, and we then weight the process that way. I mean, I have to say, very little of that is pre-planned. We do a huge amount of planning, but we don't even know what the shot sequence is going to be going into rehearsals; we don't storyboard in that sense. It is sort of storyboarding on the fly. We build a scene, dramatically, and then I work out how to shoot it. So actually, what dictates who does what amount of camera operation, or which shots and so on, is partly about what skill we discover the performers have. It's also partly about logistics, about who did the last shot, as they can't also do the next shot. And sometimes it's because a performer will say, 'I really want to do a tracking sequence here, because it's a real challenge', and they relish the physical challenge of that part of the performance. When it doesn't go so well is when people try to resist it, or hide in the dark corners of the rehearsal room going, 'I hope they don't give me any shots', and that's less successful.

JJ: I've touched on the idea that Mitchell is someone who has a very strong vision, the very strong sense of being a director in a European sense, and the publicity for those early productions often credited Katie Mitchell and the Company. However, when we come to a production which I'm sad I didn't see in Berlin, *Fräulein Julie* (2010), you're now named as the co-director, rather than the video designer. So has a shift occurred? Is it a kind of co-devised piece now?

LW: Yes, actually. I'd be interested to know when the last piece was that did say 'Devised by Katie Mitchell and the Company'. I don't remember it happening since *Waves*, interestingly.

JJ: It was used again for . . . *some trace of her* (2008). Maybe it was the early ones, 2006 to 2008?

LW: Yes, it could well have been; yes, that's interesting. I mean, where we got co-directing from was, I suppose, really an acknowledgement of (and this was an experiment, as with everything else, of acknowledging it in that way) the part that I played in the production. And actually it felt very much like a partnership; Katie would bring her extraordinary skillset, and I would bring my different skillset, shall we say, and the piece was very much a coming together of the two. It was, I would say, an unsuccessful experiment, because I'm not directing it, and she is directing it, absolutely. But it is that sort of bricolage of the visual aesthetic medium and, indeed, the shot selection and the shot construction. And, you know, it would get to the point where I was directing action, but what I wasn't directing was emotion, and of course that is what the work is.

JJ: That's her forte, yes.

LW: It may involve huge amounts of technical complexity, including how someone moves from A to B, or the manner in which they handle an object and so on, but I was not directing the emotional story and therefore that [co-director] was an erroneous term, in my opinion. Although accurate in terms of the contribution to the overall fabric of the piece, it didn't really get under the skin of it. So we've reverted. . . . I think we're still experimenting with terminology.

JJ: It's significant, isn't it, being the individual and yet being in a partnership, in a collaboration where you build trust over several years, ten years or so by now. But there isn't a term for it because I don't think multimedia theatre is quite accurate; I can't bear the term.

LW: No, I can't bear the phrase.

JJ: And it's not physical theatre. I can describe it by what it is not, but I can't tell you exactly what it is, and I think we're in that moment in collaborative endeavours where it's valuing the contributions, but it's not the right term to say 'co-directors'.

LW: No, it's not, and I do now direct as well, but it's an entirely different world and actually, I'm interested, it turns out, in different themes, and different through lines to Katie. But yes, there are a huge number of collaborators in that room on both sides of the divide, in the rehearsal room and in the auditorium and so on, who represent very long-running collaborations; sound designers, lighting designers, set designers, costume designers, but also stage management teams and the production teams that have been built. The machine exists and people get supplemented in and out and it continues to evolve. That's one of the amazing things about how Katie works. She builds these incredibly loyal teams of people who, by the intricacies of their collaboration, define what the output is. And she's very happy to acknowledge that. She's the first to give credit where it's due.

JJ: I think I may have one final thing I'd just like to touch on. What do you think her impact is in . . . well, let's just call it for the sake of argument, British theatre and culture, because of spending time outside? I just wonder what you think her impact is on the scene and younger generations coming through?

LW: It's very hard for me to say, because obviously the impact on me has been enormous, and it's quite hard to separate myself from the subjective experience of that. I think it had a huge effect on how I entered . . . well, on how I've directed a number of projects, on the direction I've taken my company in, and the collaborations that I've built there and, indeed, the work that I've now started to direct myself. In terms of cultural influence, you know, there are large numbers of people who are fascinated by the work and make requests to get archive recordings of the shows which, unfortunately, in many cases, don't really exist in any high-quality form. It's very hard to document this work, as I'm sure you've discovered, and indeed audiences who are fascinated by the form – in particular young audiences, who maybe aren't either so heavily indoctrinated in tradition or have decided, like me, that they don't particularly care about it – are now really desperate to see the work. And it's very hard to, and I very much hope that we will continue to do more of this kind of work in this country going forwards. But I don't know, I mean, I'd say a huge influence that her aesthetic interests, her thematic interests, the nature of the way she portrays emotion which, I think, is second to none, have given . . . well, I'd say a new generation but, actually, I think the influence is multi-lateral in terms of age and culture and gender; it speaks to a lot of people.

JJ: Sometimes to have something live in the imagination is not such a bad thing. Because we have to find ways of describing it. Sometimes always having the evidence doesn't help us piece it back together.

LW: No, I quite like the fact, in some cases, that the archive documentation is hard to come by, because it's nice to have it live in the memory. And it is nice, occasionally, to have the opportunity to remount things, especially old shows, because that's very interesting. It's hard to know where to draw the line in terms of whether we are recreating something, including bringing back the now antiquated video technology, for example, or whether we are accepting that things have changed. And what is the essence of some of these pieces? What is it that makes it what it is? You know, like that moment of camera cable choreography in *Waves* – I think it would be a tragedy to lose that, because that defined the nature of the machine, and the nature of the machine defines the experience to an extent. Yes, it's an interesting question.

JJ: In visual arts there is contemporary interest in how machines were historically made and worked. For example, reel-to-reel tape recorders from the 1960s, slide projectors that became redundant when PowerPoint projections were packaged in a computer, record players for vinyl rather than digital downloads, analogue radios and 16-mm film. Artists, like the 2008 Turner Prize winner, Mark Leckey, investigate how technology has transformed perceptions of and relationships to material objects and how the body relates to the machine today. It is not a seamless evolution, the relationship between art and technology; it has a disjointed and fragmented set of histories, which reminds people that this was possible then because of what was possible at a particular moment in time and history. It's still very much a construct of a moment.

LW: Yes, it is, and I sort of feel like there's no reason not to embrace the things which will make the production better, or that we might have wished to do first time around but couldn't. I don't think we've done this yet, but I also think it would be very easy to lose the essence of the work somehow.

JJ: Maybe just to round things off, then, are there particular works you want to revisit and reconfigure in some ways?

LW: There are, yes. I mean, there has been a discussion, which won't surprise you, for some years about whether we should revisit *Waves*, as the first piece. There are certain way-marker pieces over that decade or more of evolution, now, which feel particularly significant, and *Waves* is certainly one of them. I'd be very interested to revisit *Reise durch die Nacht* (2012), which is a piece that we did in Cologne originally, which is actually, probably in a sense, the most linear; it does have flashback sequences but it goes linearly through a woman's journey on a train, getting on in Paris and getting off somewhere in Austria. That was maybe the first time we did continuous film, the first more feature film–like cinematic approach. Those two in particular feel very strong, but I also feel like I could bring more to them were we to come back to them again. And, you know, thinking about how we evolve and develop into the future. . . . I mean, we don't work together so frequently any more, and there are many reasons for that. We both have many other projects going on, but actually finding the right project that really makes it worth our while to come together again to work on something is a very exciting prospect. We've discussed various ideas, and it will be interesting to see if any of them actually happen. But, as I said early on in our conversation, the idea of marrying source text with the form involves asking what is it that we're able to draw out using this form, and therefore what is the material which can be best explored. That's the question which we're constantly searching an answer to.

JJ: Well, they're very particular choices of text, aren't they? You know, they're not necessarily running off the tip of your tongue, the things you can really deconstruct and reconstruct.

LW: Yes.

JJ: I think it would be wonderful if we could see them in this country and not have to save our money. Well, we should really travel to the Continent.

LW: That would be wonderful, yes. It is very encouraging that Katie is being very much welcomed back into what you might call 'the industry' here. I mean, it certainly feels like there's less hostility towards her interests and ways of working, and the capacity for supporting the work does appear to be building again, which is great, and long may it continue.

JJ: Thank you very much, Leo, it's been a great pleasure.

LW: Thank you, it's been a pleasure.

Productions

The Seagull (2006), National Theatre (Lyttelton), London

Waves (2006), National Theatre (Cottesloe), London

Attempts on Her Life (2007), National Theatre (Lyttelton), London

. . . some trace of her (2008), National Theatre (Cottesloe), London

Wunshkonzert [*Request Programme*] (2008), Schauspiel Köln, Cologne

After Dido (2009), ENO/Young Vic, London

Fräulein Julie (2010), Schaubühne am Lehniner Platz, Berlin

Written on Skin (2012), Festival d'Aix-en-Provence, Aix-en-Provence

Reise durch die Nacht [*Night Train*] (2012), Schauspiel Köln, Cologne

The Forbidden Zone (2014), Salzburger Festspiele, Salzburg

Printed in Great Britain
by Amazon